THE COMMANDER'S EYES & EARS

In 1976 Maj. James Capers Jr. welcomed new men and their families into a force reconnaissance company. 'Only the most capable Marines are selected for this duty due to rigid mental and physical demands. A very thorough screening of each applicant is conducted . . . to test alertness and endurance. The result is a small elite unit with highly qualified Marines who are considered the best in the world'.

Indicative of the standards demanded and achieved was S.Sgt. Jimmie E. Howard's reconnaissance platoon on patrol in Vietnam in June 1966. After two days and nights of controlling artillery and air strikes on Communist forces from Hill 488, the platoon was surrounded and attacked by a battalion-size enemy force. The 18 men held out overnight in an epic small-unit action – a 'fight to remember' – in which six of their number were killed and the rest wounded. By dawn the next day the survivors were left with only eight rounds of ammunition, knives and entrenching tools. The after-action report noted that these men were average but were well trained and led, and had risen 'above normal expectations to perform an exemplary feat of arms'. Howard earned the Medal of Honor, one of six awarded to Recon Marines in Vietnam – and he was the only one who lived to wear it.

A US Marine Corps speciality is reconnaissance using amphibious and ground long-range patrols. As with many special units opinion on Marine Recon is strongly divided. Of all the American special-purpose forces it has the lowest profile. This is probably due to the Corps' desire to prevent recon from appearing as an 'elite within an elite'.

In this brief survey of recon units particular attention will be given to uniforms and equipment. Though 'reconnaissance' is as old as war, Marine Recon has a shorter history, dating from World War Two.

In 1941 the 1st Marine Division's Scout Company practiced motorized patrolling in North Carolina using M3 armoured cars. Companies like this were the first ground reconnaissance units formed. The crews wear the newly issued M41 utilities and M1 helmets. (USMC)

ORGANIZATION & OPERATIONS: WORLD WAR II

Prior to World War Two the Marine Corps developed the doctrine, equipment, and organization used for amphibious warfare in the Pacific. These efforts were first rewarded at Guadalcanal, then on Bougainville, Tarawa, New Britain, Kwajalein, Eniwetok, Saipan, Guam, Tinian, Peleiu, Iwo Jima, and Okinawa. By the end of the war the Marines had grown to include six divisions and five air wings and the Corps' strength peaked at 485,113. However, the war was not without its cost, leaving nearly 87,000 Marines dead and wounded.

The war in the Pacific began before, and continued after, the USA's involvement in the war in Europe. Much of this campaign was fought by as few as 100,000 combat troops. With the exception of the Philippines, New Guinea, and Okinawa, largely Army operations, ground fighting in the Pacific was limited to small islands, or small sections of larger islands: battlefields for which the US Navy and Marine Corps were ideally prepared. The distances the Marines travelled to do their fighting were phenomenal. The division that took Roi-Namur in the Marshall Islands, for instance, sailed 4,500 miles from its base to its objective. Several special organizations were established to meet the demands of the Pacific Theater, including units with specific tactical applications: base defence troops, paratroopers, raiders, and reconnaissance units. Most were disbanded when their functions were no longer needed; but the ground and amphibious reconnaissance units still exist in today's Marine Corps.

Amphibious and ground reconnaissance was discussed in the Marine Corps' *Small Wars Manual*; this covered long-range patrols in detail, based upon inter-war experience in Latin America. Scouting, observation, and sniping techniques were also refined by Marines on the Western Front in the First World War. The first *Tentative Landing Operations Manual* called for accurate information of landing areas, particularly beaches. Small patrols were thought to be the best way of obtaining this information. Patrols were to be made up of available naval personnel and varied in size from two to 30 men. Armed with small arms, patrols used small boats and swimmers to land agents, capture prisoners, to observe from off-shore, and to go ashore. Actions were to be at night, without air or gunfire support. In 1940 Atlantic and Pacific Fleet exercises used reconnaissance teams put ashore by submarine and seaplane in the course of amphibious landing operations. Shortly afterwards it fell to the Fleet Marine Force (FMF) to form full-time 'recon' units.

Marine Recon's reputation has been used by friends and foes alike to present contrasting public images. In fact, the actual purpose of reconnaissance units has often been ignored by both. This recruiting picture was used as Soviet propaganda. (Levadov)

EDITOR: LEE JOHNSON

OSPREY
MILITARY

ELITE SERIES

55

MARINE RECON 1940-90

Text by
CHARLES D MELSON
Colour plates by
PAUL HANNON

First published in Great Britain in 1994 by
Osprey, an imprint of Reed Consumer Books Ltd.
Michelin House, 81 Fulham Road,
London SW3 6RB
and Auckland, Melbourne, Singapore and Toronto

ISBN 1 85532 391 5

Filmset in Great Britain by Keyspools Ltd
Printed through Bookbuilders Ltd, Hong Kong

For a catalogue of all books published by Osprey Military
please write to:

**The Marketing Manager,
Consumer Catalogue Department,
Osprey Publishing Ltd,
Michelin House, 81 Fulham Road,
London SW3 6RB**

Author's dedication

In memory of two who died doing what recon does,
1st.Sgt. William G. Boyd and Cpl Bernard M.
McManus.
*. . . they will soar as with eagles' wings:
they will run and not grow weary,
walk and not grow faint.* Isaiah, 40

Acknowledgements

Thanks to Kevin Lyles, Donna Neary, Gordon
Rottman and Ray Stubbe for previous help. Specific
acknowledgements to the Marine Corps Gazette, the
Marine Corps Historical Center, Capt. A.J. Copp, Sgt.
W. Coulter, Capt. D.A. Dawson, Col. D.D. Duncan,
Sgt. A.J. Gasper, Col. J.L. Jones, J. McPherson, Maj.
M.J. Paulovich, Lt.Col. L. Rogers, Capt. J. Sandoval,
and Maj. E.J. Wages.

Publisher's note

Readers may wish to study this title in conjunction with
the following Osprey publications:
Elite 43 *Vietnam Marines 1965–73*

Artist's note

Readers may care to note that the original paintings
from which the colour plates in this book were prepared are available for private sale. All reproduction
copyright whatsoever is retained by the publisher. All
enquiries should be addressed to:

Paul Hannon
90, Station Road,
King's Langley,
Hertfordshire,
WD4 8LB

The publishers regret that they can enter into no
correspondence upon this matter.

Division Scout Companies

When the first two Marine divisions were established, each included a scout company of seven officers and 132 men in a headquarters and three platoons. Organized in March 1941, these men were trained to scout on foot, from motorcycles, and from M3 armoured cars. Subsequently these companies became part of the division's tank battalion with a motorized reconnaissance mission. On arrival in the Pacific Theater, rubber boats were issued and dismounted patrol techniques taught by old-timers with 'Banana War' experience in jungle terrain. The scout cars remained through 1942, when they were replaced by jeeps. Eventually, 'rubber boats and field shoes' became the most widely used methods of transport.

It took campaign seasoning to realize the value of combat information and how to get it through observation and patrolling. On Guadalcanal an amphibious patrol of division scouts was ambushed and wiped out while conducting a poorly prepared operation beyond friendly lines; among the dead was the 1st Marine Division's intelligence officer. Later the division commander, Gen. Alexander A. Vandegrift, recommended Robert Rogers' 1757 rules for Ranger service in Colonial North America: 'Study their tactics, fit in our modern weapons, and you have a solution' to the problems faced in the South Pacific.

Wartime necessity accelerated developments and, in January 1942, a group of specialists was formed in the Atlantic Fleet to develop amphibious reconnaissance techniques and equipment. It later went to the Pacific Fleet and formed the basis of the first amphibious reconnaissance company. In August 1942 the US Navy formed the Amphibious Scout and Raider School at Fort Pierce, Florida, to train

A patrol being transported by a New Zealand landing craft (LCPR) to scout a forward area in the South Pacific. A mix of utilities, helmets, and personal equipment are shown. The I Marine Amphibious Corps relied on patrolling by a variety of units to accomplish amphibious reconnaissance; these included Marine Raiders and Parachute battalions, whose organization, equipment, and training were suited for behind-the-line ventures. (USMC)

Right: A force-level recon unit was formed in 1943 in Hawaii. The commanding officer of the Amphibious Reconnaissance Company and his staff are photographed at Camp Catlin, wearing khaki tropical uniforms. Rank insignia are displayed on the collars and caps, along with a bronze cap badge. A mixture of belts and footwear are worn. Capt. James L. Jones, the company commander, is in the first row at left. (Jones)

individual soldiers, sailors, and Marines in raiding and patrolling techniques. The squads which evolved had three- or four-man fire teams armed with M1 Garand rifles, Thompson and Reising sub-machine guns or M1918 Browning automatic rifles. Doctrine was based on the experience accumulated from patrols led by Col. Merritt A. Edson and Col. Evans F. Carlson in Latin America, refined in China with help from Lt.Col. William E. Fairbairn, and more recent Pacific experience with the Raiders. A recon squad incorporated a sergeant squad leader and nine men, including three corporals. They trained to operate as three-man units, but in practice patrols were restricted to the size of the available rubber boats, with two-, seven-, and ten-man capacity. A four-man team is still the basis of current recon organization. By the Bougainville campaign intelligence training

and organization had paid off, and the scout companies had moved away from tank battalion employment.

A definitive operation was carried out by the 2d Scout Company in the Gilbert Islands in 1943, when it reconnoitred the remainder of Tarawa Atoll as the 2d Marine Division stormed Betio in a bloody battle. Along with an infantry battalion, rubber boat-delivered scouts searched and successfully secured the other islands in the chain and prevented any mutual support by the Japanese defenders.

Regimental Scout-Sniper Platoons

When the Marines began fighting in the South Pacific in 1942 they found that scouts, observers, and snipers were needed at regimental and battalion level as well as with division and corps. The solution was

Field uniform worn by a private for an ambush-patrol in the Pacific: M41 utilities, identification tags, M36 pistol belt with M12 and M42 first aid pouches and hand grenade; canteen and magazine pouch are worn behind. The sub-machine gun is the M1928A1 Thompson with 50-round magazine. An improvised shelter made from ponchos and ration boxes provides the backdrop. (USMC)

Right: Camouflage clothing, including reversible uniforms and helmet covers, worn during a reconnaissance-in-force. Of interest is the cartridge belt on the Marine at right with M12 first aid pouch, M10 canteen and carrier, and suspender straps. The uniform was associated with reconnaissance units and snipers, but was issued to a variety of other organizations. (USMC)

based on the experience of Col. William J. Whaling's sniper group on Guadalcanal. The excellent M1903 Springfield rifle with Weaver and Unertl telescopic sights was made available, and in 1943 a 34-man scout-sniper platoon was authorized for each infantry regiment. The key to its three squads was the two-man sniper and observer team. Scout-snipers served throughout the Pacific, but got lost in the shuffle at the end of the war. Sniping skills have since become something of a minor 'cult' in the marksmanship community.

Division Reconnaissance Companies

In May 1944 the scout companies were renamed reconnaissance companies and assigned to the division headquarters battalion, with a strength of five officers and 122 men in three platoons. 'Quite a few Marines who were assigned to the new unit came from the Parachute and Raider battalions, which were disbanded in 1944', wrote Marine Corps historian Benis M. Frank; and their influence upon techniques and equipment used by reconnaissance units was strong. The recon company became the division commander's instrument, and its duties reflected the amphibious nature of the division. Recon personnel travelled by jeep or foot on land, and by rubber boat over water when on patrol.

While trained and organized for scouting and patrolling, the reconnaissance companies were often used as independent rifle companies and for defence of division command posts. On Saipan, Recon Marines stopped a Japanese tank 'a few yards' from the 2d Marine Division commander's foxhole; and on Okinawa they fought Japanese amphibious infiltrators in the 1st Division's rear area. Recognizing the 'palace guard' relationship of the companies to the division command posts, the 4th Reconnaissance Company in the Marshalls carried out notable autonomous combat roles; and the 6th Company on Okinawa was compared to a 'private army' on a roving commission under Capt. Anthony 'Cold Steel' Walker. They often got their greatest workout after islands were secured, when by-passed enemy soldiers had to be 'mopped up'. The extensive training in scouting and patrolling paid dividends when cleaning out caves, tracking stragglers, and conducting night ambushes.

The Amphibious Reconnaissance Company

Although scout and reconnaissance companies met the needs of the division, the various Marine senior commands did not have specialized recon forces when the war began. The corps-level commands solved patrolling needs in different ways. The I Marine Amphibious Corps (later III Amphibious Corps) operated in the South Pacific, with headquarters at Guadalcanal until it moved forward to Guam. In this corps the Parachute and Raider Battalions were assigned patrols, and were well suited to behind-the-line actions. Other patrols were formed as needed from available American personnel, or with the help of Allied independent commandos and 'coastwatchers'. Active until 1943, these patrols varied in size from two to more than 40 men. Training was given in rubber boat handling, demolitions and hydrography. Specialists were included, and were put ashore by submarine, seaplane, and ship. The results obtained were as varied as the patrols themselves; some had the benefit of experienced personnel and guides familiar with the objectives; others were too large, over committed, and inexperienced. The conclusion reached was that well-planned, aggressive reconnaissance was worthwhile only if conducted by units organized, equipped, and trained for patrolling.

The V Amphibious Corps operated in the Central Pacific, with headquarters at Pearl Harbor. Its patrolling demands were met when a special unit – the Amphibious Reconnaissance Company led by Capt. James L. Jones – was formed in January 1943. Known as the 'Recon Boys', the company consisted of a headquarters and four recon platoons. A platoon of 19 men was split into two recon squads of six men each and a platoon commander with a six-man headquarters. The six-man squad, the basic patrol size, was armed with an automatic rifle, two sub-machine guns, and three rifles. A platoon could embark in two ten-man rubber boats or three seven-man boats. After nine months of training, the company was sent to the Central Pacific for operations: the Gilberts in November 1943, the Marshalls in January and February 1944, and the Marianas from June to August 1944. The company's capture of Apama Atoll with a force of 68 men was described as a 'brilliant sideshow' and model amphibious operation by the V Amphibious Corps commander.

Frequently landing at night from submarines and other vessels prior to the main assaults, the Amphibious Reconnaissance Company rendered singular service on enemy-held islands. It entered areas where 'friendly aircraft, naval gunfire, other forms of support were not available' and, under cover of darkness, moved in hostile territory under the noses of Japanese troops. The company reconnoitred some

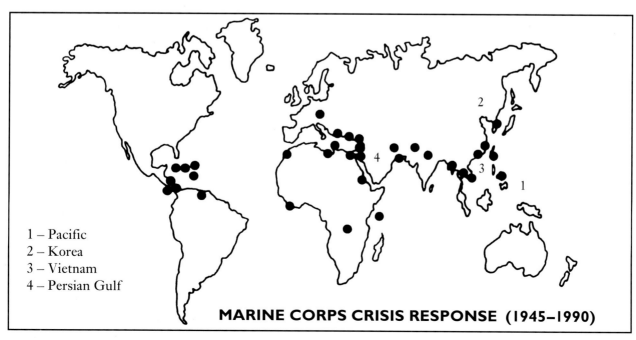

1 – Pacific
2 – Korea
3 – Vietnam
4 – Persian Gulf

MARINE CORPS CRISIS RESPONSE (1945–1990)

31 atolls, and served as a 'rifle company' during the assault on Eniwetok. After these operations – 'which occurred in rather rapid succession', wrote a company officer – it was decided to expand the company to battalion size. This expansion allowed for rotation of patrols on operations or in training, and for simultaneous missions. A larger unit would also be more able to accommodate casualties.

The Amphibious Reconnaissance Battalion

In April 1944 a two-company Amphibious Reconnaissance Battalion, with 23 officers and 291 men under Maj. J.L. Jones, was formed by the V Amphibious Corps. The companies were similar to their predecessors, with the addition of a 20-man weapons platoon armed with M1919 Browning light machine guns and 60mm mortars. The battalion moved to the Western Pacific in June 1944 for landings on Saipan and Tinian. There it operated for the first time with the US Navy's underwater demolition teams (UDT), to conduct beach reconnaissance and hydrographic surveys before and after the landings. Using combat swimmers, these missions took place at night, in unfamiliar waters, 'often through heavy surf on rocky shores'.

In February 1945 one company was sent to operate with UDT and 3d, 4th, and 5th Marine Division reconnaissance companies for the Iwo Jima landings. This mission was accomplished by the novel use of amphibious tractors. The remainder of the battalion supported the Okinawa campaign. As the only reconnaissance unit available to the Tenth Army, it infiltrated and flanked enemy positions and landed on offshore islands within the Japanese defences. In the words of Army Commander Gen. Joseph W. Stillwell, the battalion's 'aggressive action made unnecessary the use of large forces in the seizure of the Eastern Islands of Okinawa', the islands off Motobu Peninsula, and Kume Shima.

Throughout the war various structures had been tried until a balance in personnel, equipment, and employment was found: a light infantry unit of company to battalion strength. An additional requirement, wrote 1st Lt. Leo B. Shinn in 1945, was for reliable communications between patrols and transports, with 'the omnipresent necessity for rigid security measures'. One recon veteran recalled that any Marine infantry unit 'with extensive training in scouting and patrolling' could carry out recon tasks; and that all Marine rifle companies should have training in rubber boat operations for coastal raiding and reconnaissance by the division. At the lowest levels, tasks merged with scouting routines for all infantry units; but infantry units were not always available, and were not trained in specialized amphibious techniques. Clearly there was a need for Marine commanders at all levels (corps, division, regiment, and battalion) to have dedicated units equipped and trained to conduct amphibious or ground reconnaissance.

THE KOREAN WAR

The experience gained during World War Two did not survive demobilization and a shift from global war to limited conflict. Six division reconnaissance companies and a single-force reconnaissance battalion existed in 1945, but by the next year there were only two division units left. While Marine units were taking part in the post-war occupation of Japan and North China, a national defence Act established a Marine Corps of three divisions, three aircraft wings, and a reserve. This confirmed the Corps' position within the defence establishment at a minimum size in 1947. Headquarters was outside Washington, DC, and major bases were at Quantico, Virginia; Camp Lejeune, North Carolina (FMF Atlantic); Camp Pendleton, California; and throughout the Pacific region (FMF Pacific). For details see Elite 2, *The US Marine Corps*.

Even with a mandated strength, the Marines were hard pressed to field a division and air units to fight in Korea in 1950. Landing at Inchon in September, they proved that the doctrine of amphibious assault was still alive and workable. Following the recapture of Seoul the Marines advanced as far as the Chosin Reservoir where they met the Chinese Communist army as it entered the conflict. After offensives, counter-offensives, seemingly endless periods of trench warfare and occupation duty, the last Marine ground forces were withdrawn in 1955. More than 25,000 Marines were killed or wounded during the fighting. One development from the war was the use of helicopters as a means of 'vertical envelopment'.

When the war in Korea began the only available recon unit was the Reconnaissance Company, 1st Marine Division, under Capt. Kenneth J. Houghton. The company was of about the same size and organization as before; weapons included rifles, carbines, automatic rifles, and light machine guns. Recon squads operated as nine-man boat teams or changed to four-man jeep teams for motorized patrolling.

Soon after the invasion of South Korea the US Navy formed a Special Operations Group to hit the North Korean seaward flanks. The 1st Reconnaissance Company embarked with an underwater demolition team on a destroyer to launch a series of raids on Korea's east coast, destroying railroad tunnels and bridges. It also conducted hydrographic surveys on the west coast prior to amphibious landings. Operating 200 miles behind enemy lines, in confined and shallow waters, they 'inflicted important damage on shore targets'. The lack of a standing force-level reconnaissance unit was evident when the 1st Marine Division went ashore and recalled the recon company. The special operations mission went to the British Royal Marines 41 (Independent) Commando in the place of a non-existent 'force' recon unit.

After the Inchon landing the recon company screened the 1st Division's flank from Communist stragglers and partisans. On 19 September 1950 the company was first to cross the Han River. At dusk, a 13-man patrol swam over to check the far bank, while the bulk of the unit forded the river in amphibious tractors to cover the main assault. This forced the enemy to reveal their positions, and 'the crossing was made successfully'. During the battle for Seoul the recon company continued to provide flank security and hunt enemy stragglers. Later the company drew

The Korean War saw the use of equipment developed during World War Two. Capt. Kenneth J. Houghton (left), the 1st Reconnaissance Company commander, examines a tactical situation with TSgt. Ernest L. DeFazio in the summer of 1950.

Houghton wears the M41 utility uniform and DeFazio the M44 version with M1 helmet. Belts carry pouches for the M1 carbine, a leather holster with M1911 automatic pistol, and an M4 bayonet. (Duncan)

cold-weather uniforms and made the landing at Wonsan on Korea's east coast. It pushed on to Hungnam and then to the Chosin Reservoir, capturing some of the first Chinese prisoners. In freezing conditions during the subsequent fighting and withdrawal the company was in the rearguard with the division's tank battalion. In 1951 the Recon Marines conducted rear security operations with motorized patrols and roadblocks: 'all good training for new men who knew little [about reconnaissance]', commented Cpl. Paul G. Martin. That autumn, Recon Marines made the first helicopter assault in Corps history at Hill 884.

When the war began scout-sniper platoons were reactivated, with the infantry regiments using veteran regulars and reservists and available rifles, including Army-developed M1s with M80 series telescopic sights. Improved optics included the use of infrared sniper-scopes. The 1st Marine Division ran its own sniper schools to sharpen existing talent for this speciality. Little had changed from the Pacific War, and the static positions in Korea maintained the legacy of 'one shot, one kill' that kept North Koreans and Chinese off the skyline.

As the fighting continued, it increasingly became a struggle for position that left little room for motorized patrols. Large units with massed firepower overshadowed the contribution of the 118-man reconnaissance company, and combat patrols by rifle platoons and companies were used to dominate No Man's Land.

The confined battle area of the Korean Peninsula, and fighting under United Nations command, were not conducive to the reconnaissance operations that were also being performed by other agencies. The Korean War emphasized the need for force-level reconnaissance units and the limitations caused by the size of the division company. Atlantic and Pacific Fleet amphibious reconnaissance battalion cadres were activated, but did not go to Korea. Division companies needed expansion, and the disadvantages of light infantry in combat roles were recognized. The 1st Reconnaissance Company came out of the conflict with credit, being declared the 'eyes and ears of the division'.

In 1955 the reconnaissance community consisted of two division companies, two force companies, and a reserve company. The force-level units concen-

The Korean winter of 1950 required Marines to improvise cold weather clothing until sufficient types and quantities were available. This sniper wears an enlisted man's overcoat over an M43 field jacket with detachable hood. The scarf and glove inserts are wool. He is armed with an M1903 Springfield rifle. (Duncan)

trated on amphibious reconnaissance and work with underwater demolition teams, submarines, and pre-landing operations. The division units continued to train in motorized and rubber boat patrols. Progress was made in the use of helicopters, and with underwater breathing apparatus, to improve the delivery of scouts and patrols.

Force Reconnaissance Companies

In 1957 reorganization occurred, based both on Korean experience and on the projected needs of helicopter mobility in a nuclear war with the Communist bloc. The FMF Pacific and Atlantic amphibious reconnaissance companies were redesignated 1st and 2d Force Reconnaissance Companies. The table of organization was 14 officers and 149 men in headquarters, service, amphibious recon, airborne

In 1952, at Hyonam-Dong, members of the 1st Reconnaissance Company rehearse for an ambush wearing M44 camouflage utilities and sage green utility caps. The extremes of Korean climate required both hot and cold weather clothing depending upon the season. Visible weapons are M1A1 sub-machine guns, and M2 carbines with magazine pouches on the buttstocks; no other personal equipment is evident. (USMC)

recon, and pathfinder platoons. The latest parachute, diving and rubber boat technology was adopted, with light armament consisting of sub-machine guns and pistols. The image engendered by these units was one of the 'New Marines', with the mission of conducting pre- and post-assault 'deep reconnaissance', and helicopter guidance for their commanders.

Division Reconnaissance Battalions

In 1958 the division companies were expanded to battalion size, with 29 officers and 491 men in headquarters and service and recon companies. Armament was increased with rifles, carbines, pistols, automatic rifles, light machine guns, rocket launchers, and light mortars. The division units had a strong 'Raider' tradition, conducting 'distant' ground reconnaissance and observation for the division commander by means of foot, vehicle, and helicopter-mobile patrols.

Unlike previous organizations neither recon unit was assigned combat missions for which it was not equipped. Great emphasis was placed on radio reporting of information to higher headquarters 'in an amphibious operation under threat of nuclear attack against a sophisticated enemy using conventional warfare'. The Fleet Marine Force operated principally in areas that precluded the use of motorized forces, and placed a premium on light infantry with supporting arms. This resulted in ground reconnaissance, with an emphasis on foot patrolling and helicopter mobility. Pure information-gathering was stressed, covert rather than overt reconnaissance – getting in and out undetected. In a study of Robert Rogers in 1961 historian John R. Cuneo made a strong comparison between the new recon units and the French–Indian War Rangers. This affinity was strengthened by Recon Marines' attendance at the coveted US Army Ranger School.

The Cold War turned into a Counter-Insurgency Era, with numerous 'hot' conflicts that stopped short of general or even limited wars. Events showed that in insurgent warfare threats were against base areas in unconventional situations, by 'relatively unsophisticated forces employing guerrilla tactics'. In July 1958 a brigade-size force landed in Lebanon to restore order. During the Cuban Missile Crisis in October 1962 a large amphibious force was gathered; this included force and division recon, and reconnaissance teams that were deployed but not landed. In 1963 Marines responded to other emergencies in Laos and Haiti.

With this experience, and internal debate reflecting a renewed focus on 'special' forces and warfare[1], improvements were made to both recon organizations in 1963. Force reconnaissance companies were changed, they were to consist of six recon platoons with identical missions. Each platoon

[1] The US Navy sea, air, land (SEAL) teams were formed in 1962 from UDT cadres when the Corps decided it had all the units it needed for counter-insurgency, long a Marine speciality.

THE VIETNAM WAR

Camouflage utilities are worn by two Recon Marines in 1958, with amphibious gear laid out for display, including a rubber boat (IBL). By this date units had been organized and developed to support both force and division commanders.

This was due to increased interest on the part of senior officers, such as Gen. Randolph M. Pate, Commandant of the Marine Corps, shown here inspecting 2d Force Reconnaissance Company in North Carolina. (USMC)

The landing of the 9th Marine Expeditionary Brigade at Da Nang in March 1965 marked the start of large-scale involvement in Vietnam. The III Marine Amphibious Force strength rose to a peak of about 85,000 during the 1968 Tet offensive. The Marine withdrawal began in 1969, as the South Vietnamese began to assume a larger role in the fighting; the large ground units, and recon, were out of Vietnam by June 1971. The Vietnam War, the longest in the history of the Marine Corps, exacted a high cost: over 14,000 Marines killed and more than 88,000 wounded.

The 1st and 3d Reconnaissance Battalions and the 1st and 3d Force Reconnaissance Companies supported their respective division and force commanders in South Vietnam's I Corps area. Marine Recon had to find a (sometimes) elusive enemy, and in doing so were nicknamed the 'Green Ghosts' by the Communists. Very soon after their arrival, the first Medal of Honor awarded to a Marine during the war went to a platoon leader with the 3d Reconnaissance Battalion, 1st Lt. Frank S. Reasoner, who died helping his radio man to cover while ambushed on 12 July 1965.

Reconnaissance operations were conducted in the most northerly of the South Vietnamese military regions bordering Laos, North Vietnam, and the South China Sea. The enemy were both North Vietnamese Army regulars prosecuting conventional warfare, and 'Viet Cong' guerrillas operating clandestinely in populated areas. From the west, valleys and ridges served as infiltration routes for Communists attacking coastal bases, and these same hinterlands serve as their own rear areas. Recon units conducted deep and distant patrols to detect the location of Communist forces in support of combat, security, and pacification programmes by the South Vietnamese and Allied forces. Lt.Gen. Bernard E. Trainor, then commanding 1st Reconnaissance Battalion, described these patrols as being made up of seven-man 'recon teams', with a point man, team leader, corpsman, two radiomen, a grenadier, and 'tail-end Charlie'. He felt that much of the conduct of

was made up of an officer and 14 men, in three teams of four. The division reconnaissance battalion was to be made up of 32 officers and 438 men in four companies, and the loss of air control parties and crew-served weapons. Its platoons were larger, with an officer and 23 men in two recon squads of two teams of four men each. The M14 rifle, M79 grenade launcher, and M60 machine gun came into use, although the M3 sub-machine gun was retained in force recon. Assignments remained the same; Marines felt that this structure was sound for both conventional and unconventional warfare. In 1965 an amphibious brigade landed in the Dominican Republic to protect American citizens and evacuate those who wished to leave; and a reconnaissance platoon conducted a pioneering night helicopter pathfinder operation.

the mission 'was tied to well-rehearsed and practiced drills'.

Maj.Gen. Raymond G. Davis, a Marine division commander, wrote that between 1968 and 1969 less than 40% of his area was secured by combat forces, and the rest was 'covered by reconnaissance' by patrols from 3d Force Recon Company and 3d Recon Battalion. These were either combat patrols, within the 70% of the division area covered by artillery; or recon patrols, in the outer reaches 'beyond friendly artillery range'. Radio communication was vital, and patrols were eventually in constant contact with headquarters to co-ordinate support. Two radios per patrol was normal, the radio being worth more than any other item of equipment; coupled with a high volume of small arms fire in case of ambush, it provided the key to survival. The effective use of 'insertion and extraction packages' of attack, transport helicopters and observation aircraft were innovations well suited to Vietnam. For example the special-patrol-insertion-and-extraction 'rig' used to lift teams out of areas where there was no landing zone proved invaluable. Rubber boats, parachutes, and SCUBA were not needed to any great extent; recon specialist Lt.Col. George W. 'Digger' O'Dell

recalled that 'the two means usually employed were helicopter inserts or walking'.

Both recon and combat patrols of just under a week's duration were used to make contact with the enemy, and were then exploited by a rapid build-up of infantry forces or air and artillery fire. In locations where large-scale operations were not conducted recon served as an economy-of-force measure, with 'Keyhole' recon patrols used to obtain information on Communist units, bases, and movements. These were small (four to ten men), lightly armed, and dependent upon stealth to accomplish their tasks. 'Stingray' combat patrols were organized to make contact with enemy forces through ambush or supporting fire. Larger than recon patrols (eight to 12 men), these were more heavily armed, and dependent upon aggressive operations to get in and out of enemy areas. As an example, one of these patrols used 12 artillery missions and 15 air strikes to kill 204 enemy. Over the period of a year, one force and division recon combination conducted 1,333 patrols, supported 22 battalion-size or larger operations, and accounted for 2,683 enemy casualties. In addition, patrols captured prisoners, located downed aircraft crews, placed electronic sensors, wire-tapped communications, and manned radio-relay stations. A well-known US Army officer, Col. David H. Hackworth, felt that Marine Recon 'enjoyed phenomenal success and were considered by many similar Army units as the best in the business'.

Early on, the III Marine Amphibious Force had assigned the force reconnaissance companies to work with the recon battalions. All were employed to gather and report information and to use supporting arms as economy-of-force measures. This merged missions to some degree, and the lack of structure caused friction until a force-level surveillance and reconnaissance centre was established to co-ordinate and disseminate all information gathering by Marines.

The Vietnam War validated and refined the force and division reconnaissance concepts, particularly

Parachuting was adopted by force recon units, including experimental free fall methods to insert scouts and pathfinders to assist helicopter assaults. These Marines conduct a 'hop and pop' training jump in North Carolina in 1960, wearing black football-type helmets, leather boots, and utilities. (USMC)

for battalion recon, which expanded to six companies (with a force recon company and an extra company within each battalion). Force recon met the demands of combat, but was limited by the amphibious force area of operations and the presence of other services and joint forces conducting corresponding missions (the unconventional warfare task force), in some cases using similar doctrine and techniques.

In a replay of World War Two and Korea, scout–sniper platoons were mobilized within the infantry regiments, and a 31-man platoon existed in the reconnaissance battalions by 1966. Winchester and Remington 7.62mm rifles with Unertl or Redfield telescopic sights were used – later referred to as the M40 system. Optics were perfected with 'starlight' scopes, range finders, and laser target designators. Two-man teams were still used, and sniping compensated for the range limitations of the standard issue M16 rifle. Snipers provided harassment and observation assistance rather than specific targeted liquidations. The published record for Vietnam snipers was 93 confirmed kills, including one almost unbelievable 2,000-yard shot. Despite their usefulness, both the regimental and recon sniper platoons faded away again at the end of the Vietnam War.

Other American units had an impact and influ-

Parachuting brought new techniques and equipment. This Marine wears a jump helmet, M44 camouflage utilities, Corcoran boots and a modified T10 parachute. The layout includes a K-Bar knife with flare, camera, radio generator, signal lamp, rations, M3 sub-machine gun, binoculars and M41 personal equipment. (USMC)

Platoon from 3d Reconnaissance Battalion at Chu Lai, Vietnam, in 1965. Weapons are M14 rifles, with some modified examples, and M1A1 submachine guns. This early period was marked by a variety of uniforms, including M58, M62, 'tiger-stripes', and early jungle utilities, with differing headgear. (Sandoval)

ence on Marines in Vietnam, including the US Army 'Black Beret' long range reconnaissance and Ranger patrols (LRRP) at the brigade and division level, and the 'Green Beret' Special Forces which provided recon teams for the commander-in-chief. The Military Advisory Command Vietnam had a school teaching prevailing reconnaissance methods, the

Right: Reconnaissance and surveillance skills continued to be the mainstay of recon units, with division stressing ground patrolling, and force concentrating on pathfinder and amphibious patrols.

Pictured in 1964, a 2d Marine Division corporal mans an observation post with M49 spotting scope, M38 document case, and wearing the M44 camouflage utility uniform. (USMC)

Left: Deployment to Vietnam began with beach and port studies by 1st Force Reconnaissance Company and Navy Underwater Demolition Teams. These were largely 'administrative' missions, but the first Recon Marine killed in Vietnam was engaged on a beach survey in 1965. Here rubber boats (IBS) are launched at China Beach near Da Nang; the scouts wear standard olive green swimming trunks, and use standard troop life vests. (USMC)

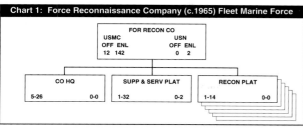

	FOR RECON CO		
	USMC OFF ENL 12 142	USN OFF ENL 0 2	
CO HQ 5-26 0-0	SUPP & SERV PLAT 1-32 0-2	RECON PLAT 1-14 0-0	

Chart 2: Reconnaissance Battalion (c.1965) Marine Division

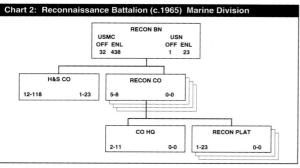

	RECON BN		
	USMC OFF ENL 32 438	USN OFF ENL 1 23	
H&S CO 12-118 1-23	RECON CO 5-8 0-0		
	CO HQ 2-11 0-0	RECON PLAT 1-23 0-0	

Organization Tables, c.1965

Below: Demands in Vietnam were varied, and included working among civilians – which made covert patrolling difficult. The 1st Marine Division scout at left displays characteristic camouflage bush hat, utilities, and jungle boots as worn by force and division recon during the middle years of the war. He carries a PRC25 radio in an 'ARVN' rucksack, and is armed with an M16 rifle with a rappelling rope as a sling. (USMC)

MACV Recondo School at Nah Trang; Marines used this, and other service schools, to refine and broaden their own methods. The essentially advisory nature of the conflict found Recon Marines assigned to the Republic of Vietnam Armed Forces, including the Vietnamese Marine Corps, the Special Operations Group, and the Civil Operations Revolutionary Development Support. Assignment called for personnel with experience in reconnaissance, special warfare, and special operations to advise units that used these skills in internal and external missions. Though few in number, these Marines shared recon expertise with the different special warfare forces. Even the Communists had reconnaissance units, noting that it took over a year to train a recon man (the Marines claimed that it was two years). These were encountered by Marine patrols, as were the more numerous 'trackers' who watched potential landing zones and tailed patrols, and the more aggressive 'killer team' counter-reconnaissance detachments in the Communist rear.

The lessons of this war confirmed those of earlier conflicts, and added new techniques to the concept of reconnaissance, calling for teams that could 'shoot, move, and communicate', in order to survive and accomplish their assignments. The dynamic use of

recon teams as small independent action forces to engage the enemy with fire support provided an element of combat power previously lacking, but had the effect of limiting their core information-gathering effort. The balance of combat and intelligence responsibilities was tested, and left unresolved, in favour of a mix of both. Marine Recon provided the force and division commanders with timely and accurate information on the enemy and its area of operations that could not be obtained any other way. Lt.Col. O'Dell concluded that Recon Marines 'took the war to the enemy in the most personal sense', denying the Communists rest, resupply, and reinforcements. Flexibility in recon tactics was more important than any specific accomplishment. It was assumed, in post-war studies, that the requirement for force and division reconnaissance units would continue in the future despite advances in aerial photography, sensors, and other means of information gathering. Vietnam influenced recon thinking for some time afterwards, with little or no change in organization, equipment, or doctrine.

THE 1970s & 1980s

The Low-Intensity Conflict Era of the 1970s and 1980s provided worldwide employment for Marines and reconnaissance units at a low level. These confrontations matched various threats, and recon assisted in detachment strength: normally a battalion landing team had a division recon platoon, while a force recon platoon was assigned to the next highest command element. This began with the October War crisis in the Middle East in 1973; and subsequently Recon Marines aided in the evacuation of US citizens and foreign nationals during unrest in Cyprus and Lebanon in 1974. The next year saw Marines evacuating embassy staffs, American citizens and refugees from Phnom Penh, Cambodia, and Saigon, Republic of Vietnam. Later, in May 1975, Marines played an integral role in the rescue of the crew of the SS *Mayaquez* captured off the coast of Cambodia; the landing on Koh Tang Island was made without advance forces.

Scout-sniper platoons existed within infantry regiments and battalion recon units. Teams worked both in conjunction with observation posts or deployed with units for operations. This 3d Marine Division sniper and spotter are in action in 1968 at Khe Sanh. The weapon is the M40 sniper rifle; note also the M55 body armour. (Duncan)

Deep Reconnaissance Platoons

The end of the fighting in South-East Asia brought expanding responsibilities despite a reduction in defence spending. In July 1974 force recon was reduced to one regular company, and division decreased to three companies in each battalion. To compensate for the lack of force reconnaissance assets, a 23-man deep reconnaissance platoon was formed in the 1st and 3d Battalions in March 1975. The basic recon unit remained the four-man team: a team leader, assistant team leader, scout-radio operator, and scout-driver. Force recon had 15-man platoons and division recon 24-man platoons. Small arms were the M16 service rifle, M203 grenade launcher, and M60 machine gun.

The Marine Corps assumed an increasingly significant role on NATO's northern and southern flanks in the 1970s, as units of the II Marine Amphibious Force participated in exercises throughout Europe and the Mediterranean. The Corps also played a key role in the development of the Rapid Deployment Force, later the US Central Command, a multi-service arrangement created to ensure a flexible and timely military response to South-West Asian obligations. The Maritime Prepositioning Ships (MPS) concept was developed to enhance this by staging equipment needed for combat in the vicinity of the area of operations, reducing response

For patrolling recon Marines dispensed with the helmet and armoured vest of conventional combat units. This corporal exhibits an individual load of water, ammunition, gas mask, and grenades as worn by 3d Force Reconnaissance Company in 1969. His pack is off, but his M56 fighting equipment remains on – a prudent practice in enemy territory. He wears a locally made bush hat, and grease-paint. (USMC)

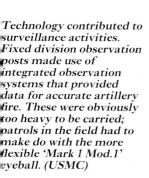

Technology contributed to surveillance activities. Fixed division observation posts made use of integrated observation systems that provided data for accurate artillery fire. These were obviously too heavy to be carried; patrols in the field had to make do with the more flexible 'Mark 1 Mod.1' eyeball. (USMC)

time as Marines travelled by air to link up with MPS material. As a result reconnaissance units arrived in conflict areas with the major combat units and not before them.

Diverse developments were brought together during this period: arctic and desert expertise was needed for new geographic areas of commitment, and jungle expertise remained important. There was renewed emphasis on amphibious reconnaissance, particularly the forward deployment of recon detachments with amphibious ready groups – the landing ships at sea in different parts of the world with embarked Marine forces. This led to more work with Navy UDTs (and later SEALs) in advance-force operations[2].

From 1976 hostage recovery programmes were started in conjunction with federal law enforcement agencies and Army Special Forces; these developed into direct action missions for some units. Motorized patrolling was stressed, and its potential for desert operations was improved with the Rapid Deployment Force for South-West Asia. The M151 jeep evolved, with modifications, into a fast attack vehicle (FAV), and continued to be used after the adaptation of the M998 high mobility multi purpose vehicle, the 'Hummer'. Scout-snipers were resurrected in 1977, with trained snipers put into infantry and recon units

armed with an improved M40 rifle and M10 telescopic sight (regimental sniper platoons were still for wartime only). Up-to-date training emphasized 'stalk and hide' techniques which fitted well with the outlook of recon scout-snipers; and new optics were developed using passive-light and heat imagers. Sniper teams had opportunities in Lebanon, Grenada, and Panama to 'reach out and touch someone'. In the Persian Gulf the Barrett M82 .50 calibre rifle was acquired for very long range sniping.

The 1980s brought an increasing number of terrorist attacks on US embassies and similar targets around the world. In the face of this challenge, the Department of Defense directed in 1981 that special operations be 'revitalized'. Indirectly this helped the Marines and recon, so that by the end of the decade manpower, equipment, and training had attained new heights. In August 1982 Marine units landed at Beirut, Lebanon, as part of the multi-national force. For the next 19 months these units faced the hazards of a peace-keeping mission with courage and professionalism (a recon platoon was lost in the suicide truck-bombing of the US Marine base). In October 1983 Marines were more successful than some other elements in the short-notice intervention in Grenada. Operation 'Urgent Fury' provided the background for Clint Eastwood's fictional recon platoon in the movie *Heartbreak Ridge*, which showcased uniforms, equipment and training.

[2] In 1983 the SEALs assimilated the UDTs and their functions.

By the time the Marines left Vietnam recon units had evolved tactics that both carried the war to the enemy and covered vital base areas. This group, from 1st Reconnaissance Battalion in Da Nang in 1970, has just returned from patrol. (Gasper)

Recon Marines served as advisers with the RVN forces, including the Vietnamese Marine Corps, which had brigade reconnaissance companies. 'Tiger-stripe' utilities were worn, with service emblems on the green beret and right breast. (USMC)

Special Operations Capable Recon

In 1985 the Marines, with the amphibious ready groups, were prepared to assume special operations 'capabilities' through training and mission focus. Tasks centred on the security requirements of a decade of low intensity conflict. Raids, hostage recovery, non-combat evacuations, and humanitarian efforts were the 'selective' maritime special operations' emphasized, according to recon expert Lt.Col. Dennis R. Blankenship. Marine Recon did not come under the joint special operations structure, although individual Marines were assigned to these commands, and close relations exist. In May 1987, an additional force reconnaissance company was activated; and in October 1988 force recon was expanded to ten platoons, assigned to either deep reconnaissance or direct action tasks. Under command of a lieutenant-colonel, force recon became a 228-man company. New weapons for division and force recon included the M16A2 rifle, M249 squad automatic rifle, M203 grenade launcher, M60E light machine gun, and M9 pistol.

Numerous other changes in defence structure and the world situation had an impact on Marine Recon units. The fleet anti-terrorism security teams with the naval security forces expanded the options against terrorist attacks. The General Motors light armoured vehicle (LAV25) 'out-motorized' jeep- and Hummer-mounted division recon in mobile patrolling, and out-gunned them for cavalry missions. The establishment of surveillance-reconnaissance-intelligence groups (SRIG) combined a number of units, and ran the surveillance and reconnaissance centre which co-ordinated assignments. This occurred against a background of technological change; electronic information-gathering was better understood than amphibious and ground patrolling. Some reconnaissance activities were strengthened and others were reduced; but, essentially, Marine Recon was in the best shape to meet the challenges to come.

In 1988 recon teams supporting naval and joint task forces 'took down' Iranian oil platforms during the 'Tanker War' in the Persian Gulf. Marines were summoned to respond to instability in Central America, when Operation 'Just Cause' was launched in Panama in December 1989. By 1990 amphibious and ground reconnaissance units in the Fleet Marine Force included two force reconnaissance companies, with two in reserve. The Marine divisions had three reconnaissance battalions and one in reserve. In this year the Iraqi invasion of Kuwait led to the largest movement of Marine Corps forces since World War Two.

THE GULF WAR

Between August and December 1990, some 24 infantry battalions, 40 air squadrons, and more than 92,000 Marines were deployed to the Persian Gulf as part of the I Marine Expeditionary Force. Operation 'Desert Storm' was launched on 16 January 1991, the same day that the air battle began. The ground attack began on 24 February when the 1st and 2d Marine Divisions, supported by the 3d Marine Aircraft Wing, breached Iraqi defence lines and stormed into Kuwait. At the same time, the hovering threat from two Marine brigades at sea nearby held some 50,000 Iraqis in check along the Kuwaiti coast. By the morning of 28 February, 100 hours after the ground battle started, almost the entire Iraqi army in Kuwait and adjacent areas of Iraq was encircled, with 4,000 tanks destroyed and 42 divisions destroyed or rendered ineffective.

With the I Marine Expeditionary Force was the 1st Force Reconnaissance Company, reinforced with detachments from the 2d, 3d, and 4th Companies. The 1st and 2d Reconnaissance Battalions, and elements of the 3d Battalion, served with the two divisions ashore and the two brigades at sea. Initially, observation posts were set up along the Kuwaiti border and motorized patrols were conducted by force and division recon teams. Facilitated by satellite communications, digital terminals, and global positioning systems, these teams were tasked with 'scouting the forward edge of enemy lines and division routes'. Prior to the ground offensive, reconnaissance patrols took some 238 prisoners.

Recon units engaged in combat early, and the Iraqi advance into Khafji in January 1991 by-passed several patrols in the town, where they continued to call artillery and air down on Iraqi armour. Division reconnaissance units were assigned to the mechanised task forces formed for the ground offensive, with duties including identifying obstacles and navigating routes through the fortified lines established to defend Kuwait. Army Gen. H. Norman Schwarzkopf reported to the Chairman of the Joint Chiefs of Staff that for a week, Marines 'from the reconnaissance units have been crawling through all that stuff. They've been crawling all night and hiding all day, and they have penetrated all the way through'. Given the Marines' success in passing through minefields, wire, and obstacles to mark lanes for the attack, Schwarzkopf felt that 'when the ground war begins it will be like Broadway'. A final note: on 26 February 1991 an advance patrol from 2d Force Reconnaissance Company drove up to the abandoned US Embassy in Kuwaiti City, guided by Kuwait resistance fighters, just ahead of the Special Forces assigned to liberate the embassy complex.

Swift, Silent, Deadly

Overshadowed by the Gulf War were a number of other events demonstrating the Corps' flexible and rapid response. These included evacuations in Liberia and Somalia to rescue diplomats and civilians, and humanitarian efforts in Bangladesh, the Philippines, and Northern Iraq. These actions brought changes and new employment for recon. The differences between the two types of Marine reconnaissance units and their roles were highlighted. Force recon was bolstered, while the division structure was challenged by the need for manoeuvre

Desert camouflage utilities, acquired in 1982, worn by a communications instructor. Improved radio techniques and equipment were available by the Gulf War in 1990, including the lightweight PRC104 high-frequency radio, burst transmission equipment, satellite terminals, and capabilities for formatted message traffic.

regiments to have mobile recon units in direct support. The management advantage of the SRIG was inhibited by the mixing of personnel, and by a reliance on technical collection of intelligence that neglected ground reconnaissance. The 1990s appeared to be another period of change for Marine Recon after their recent war and peacekeeping endeavours.

The 50-year milestone finds recon units in a state of transition, and in the position of preparing for the next war with limited budgets – the modern military dilemma. In a reversal of the Vietnam era, when division-level recon was emphasized, the stress is now placed on the force reconnaissance unit in direct action as a special operations unit. Division recon is undergoing reconsideration, and has yet to find a satisfactory solution. Typically, some commands have changed while others retain the force and division reconnaissance structure that has served for more than 30 years. The patrolling watchword – Don't believe anything you hear, and only half of what you see' – should also be remembered by 'recon-watchers' trying to follow these evolutions.

Recon doctrine, organization, and utilization ultimately depend on the terrain and situation, which alone determine what can be accomplished.

The stormy relationship between the Marine Corps and its recon units illustrates a dynamic process, described by Lt.Col. Don P. Wycoff in 1963 as the 'super soldier' selection-rejection cycle. This cycle, common to most modern armies, sees a build-up of special forces followed by a predictable decline. Part of the dilemma of Marine Corps reconnaissance units is the lack of a 'sponsor' with any authority; and the separation of personnel, organizational, and equipment decisions between local commanders. Even the formal distinction between force and divi-

By 1991, 1st Force Reconnaissance Company had obtained the vehicle used by other special operations elements in the Persian Gulf, the Chenowth light strike vehicle. Marine versions were painted desert tan while those of other services were all black, *like this example in Kuwait City. The cargo and weapons load consisted of a Mk19 grenade launcher, M60 machine guns, and AT4 anti-tank missiles. Desert camouflage uniforms are worn with rain suits, ALICE gear, and PASGT body armour.*

sion units rests largely on tradition and personalities – they are, after all, the same people with a common culture. Recon's own self-centred view is expressed in the belief that there are only two types of Marines: 'those who are in recon, and those who want to be'.

At present one cannot enter the Corps strictly for reconnaissance duty; officers and enlisted men must first complete basic training and earn a speciality, normally infantry or communications. Assignment to a reconnaissance unit is predicated on being physically qualified for parachute and diving duty; volunteering; passing unit screening; and completing indoctrination training. Attendance at amphibious reconnaissance, Army airborne, and Navy dive courses are general qualifications to produce a 'Reconnaissance Man', and other qualifications such as Ranger or scout-sniper are highly desirable. The one constant is that in the age of mass produced fighting men and firepower, Marine reconnaissance units continue to champion individual skills and teamwork, aided but not replaced by technology.

In one form or another, the commander's need to rely on a small group of trained men to accomplish special tasks continues, whether for small independent action missions or reconnaissance. As long as this necessity exists, then there is the need for Marine Recon. Fred Reed, a reporter and former Marine, once asked why a 'crazy outfit' like recon existed; the reply was that 'all things are possible to those who refuse to be reasonable', and if you were going to do something, 'you might as well try to be the best at it'.

UNIFORMS & ACCOUTREMENTS

Generally, recon units have used the uniforms common throughout the Marine Corps, though local availability, style, and access to other services' items have also had an impact. While not subject to precise documentation, this summary will consider uniforms and insignia that have evolved since 1940. A 1950s handbook stated that Marine reconnaissance units were provided with 'basic infantry equipment and small arms', plus certain special equipment listed as inflatable boats, survival kits, and instruments to measure and record data. In general no special uniforms were required, except for gloves, canvas shoes, swimming clothing, and exposure suits in cold water. It was noted that all items should be 'light, durable, and waterproof'.

In matters of style, there have been two extremes in recon dress: the 'spit shine' versus the 'fluff and buff' syndrome. This was illustrated in the dress observed in the amphibious and pathfinder platoons – the former in the relaxed style of navy underwater demolition teams, and the latter reflecting the more demanding fashion of the army airborne. Carried to extremes, both emphasized appearance over performance, the true constant which defines uniforms and equipment for reconnaissance units. Despite regulation, variety flourished concurrently within the same theatres of operations, and depended upon the supervision exercised.

While patrolling has been described as long periods of boring routine with moments of sheer terror or exhilarating payback, living conditions out of action could range from a cot in a squad tent with twelve or more other people; canvas and wood 'strong-back' tents; Quonset huts; or tin-roofed 'South-East Asia' huts. Even shipboard life for the Marines serving with amphibious landing forces was an improvement, as they were dry, and well fed by

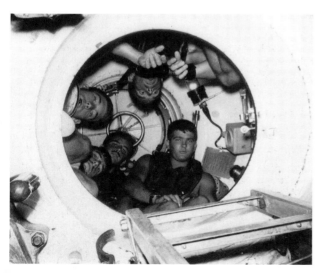

Combat swimmers inside the escape trunk rehearse exit procedures; this was done without diving equipment, as more men could be put out if they used buoyant ascent techniques without the burden of breathing gear. Once on the surface they would swim, or inflate rubber boats, for the trip to the beach. (USMC)

the US Navy while aboard ship. One veteran of both reconnaissance and infantry units commented that at least in recon one rotated patrols, and had time in between to rest and relax before going out again; in the infantry 'you went out and stayed out'.

Other recon-qualified Marine advisers served with the Military Advisory Command and the maritime commandos of the Special Operations Group, which conducted raids and reconnaissance along the Vietnamese coast. Shown in Da Nang in 1970, this team wear ARVN camouflage, the red ARVN Airborne beret, and a distinctive unit emblem on the right breast. Weapons include AK-47 assault rifles, M45 sub-machine guns and M79 grenade launchers. (USMC)

Insignia and Markings

World War Two rank insignia were gold or silver metal pin-on shirt collar and coat shoulder strap emblems for officers. Enlisted chevrons were worn on service uniforms including the M41 field jacket, but none were worn on the utility uniform; this led to the use of hand-drawn black paint or ink insignia on the jacket sleeves, utility cap and helmet cover. Similar expedient rank insignia were used through the Korean War, and marking stencils were issued. After Korea removable blackened brass enlisted collar insignia were adopted, and a similar version is in use today. In 1959 the present enlisted structure was established, with crossed M1 rifles being added at the base of the chevrons. Vietnam and Persian Gulf-era rank insignia were of a metal or synthetic pin-on type, with black chevrons for enlisted ranks and bright silver or gold for officers. Insignia were worn on both collars, if at all, in the field. Enlisted rank was

worn at an angle to the front edge of the collar, and officer rank centred and parallel to the front collar edge.

Various gold and silver metal individual qualification badges ('wings'), mainly for aviation skills, were worn over the left shirt and jacket pocket. As a matter of course, Marines did not adopt speciality badges or emblems. Distinctions that originated during World War Two included the US Army's parachute badge for Fort Benning-trained Marines. Other devices were the rare special forces brevet of the Office of Strategic Services, and US Navy parachute rigger insignia – either cloth sleeve rate or the little-known metal breast insignia based on the naval aviation 'wings'.

The Navy-Marine Corps parachutist insignia was approved in 1963 and initially awarded to force reconnaissance personnel. It was intended to be a proficiency badge indicating advanced recon training, but it was also earned by other Marine and Navy personnel with less demanding assignments. Parachute insignia, particularly the 'gold wings', were actually awarded by pounding the pin fasteners into the Marine's chest as 'blood' wings, christened with liberal amounts of beer. The 2d Class Diver badge 'bubble head' was authorized for wear in 1974. The recipients of both parachutist and diver insignia are considered 'dual-qualified' (or 'dual-cool') full-fledged 'Reconnaissance Marines'.

The Marines emphasize service rather than unit loyalty. To enhance this, insignia were not worn other than the Corps emblem found on the cap and combat uniforms. This used a traditional eagle, globe and anchor insignia stencilled on the left breast pocket by the manufacturer; from 1941, this was a 1936 branch-of-service emblem with the initials 'USMC'. It eventually found its way to the utility and helmet covers. Bronze cap badges were worn on the garrison 'overseas' cap, fibre 'tropical' helmet, M1 helmet liner, and examples are also seen on the utility cap. The 1954 branch-of-service emblem came into effect on the M56 utilities. By the Vietnam era most utility shirts were issued unmarked with a service emblem, the individual used heat transfer or stencils to apply them to the shirt. With unit replacement of clothing in Vietnam these 'USMC Transfers' were not always available. The field jacket, being unit property, was seldom marked like this.

Formation insignia for Marines had antecedents in World War One, when Marines served in the US Army's 2d Infantry Division; and from the defence of Iceland in 1941, where the British 49th Division's polar bear sign was presented as a courtesy. Between 1943 and 1947 'battle blazes' were worn, beginning with the 1st Marine Division's sleeve insignia. These consisted of multi-coloured embroidered insignia or 'patches' sewn to the upper left sleeve as unit identification on overcoats, field jackets, service jackets, and shirts. Division recon companies wore the insignia for the 1st to the 6th Marine Divisions, while the amphibious recon unit wore the emblem for the V Amphibious Corps and later Fleet Marine Force Pacific. The Raider's death's-head and the Paramarine's parachute canopy continued in various forms, with informal emblems based on the World War Two motifs; these could be found on clothing, equipment, signs, plaques, and other informal items.

More unimaginative unit identification came to being in World War Two with the use of embarkation or tactical markings. This was a practice initially reserved for equipment, reflecting the 'indus-

USMC INSIGNIA OF GRADE

General

Lieutenant General

Major General

Brigadier General

Colonel (Right)   Colonel (Left)

Lieutenant Colonel   Major

Captain   First Lieutenant   Second Lieutenant

CWO W-4   CWO W-3   CWO W-2   WO W-1

Sergeant Major of the Marine Corps   Sergeant Major   Master Gunnery Sergeant   First Sergeant

Master Sergeant   Gunnery Sergeant   Staff Sergeant

Sergeant   Corporal   Lance Corporal   Private 1st Class

'trial' approach to amphibious operations under which everyone and everything had its place in the landing plan. By 1943 these markings were seen on clothing and individual equipment. They consisted of a stencilled geometric shape with a series of three to four coded numerals. The shape indicated the command: a horizontal diamond for the 1st Marine Division, a square for the 2d, a vertical diamond for the 3d, an upper half-circle for the 4th, a rectangle for the 5th, and a circle for the 6th. The numerals identified unit, sub-unit, and in some cases even rank. Variations of these 'tac-marks' are still used on equipment, vehicles, and supplies.

An individual was required to mark his personal items with his name at designated places on the uniform. This was generally done with a stamp or stencil in black block letters over the left chest pocket, and inside the waist band of the trousers. More obvious name placement was used overseas above the left pocket, on the pocket, and across the back of the jacket. These stampings could include the nine-digit social security number or the older seven-digit service number. The markings served the practical purpose of identifying individual equipment, even though this was not sanctioned. A Marine's last initial and the last four numbers of his social security number were used to identify his web gear, a unique method employed as personalizing government property was frowned upon. Mistakes or changes

were blotted out with ink, which made for messy uniforms. Utilities worn by the first Marine units to arrive in Vietnam had embroidered name tags over the left breast pocket for those deploying from Okinawa. During the Vietnam War cloth name tapes were used informally, these bore last names and unit designations (i.e. '3d Force Recon' or 'U.S. Marines').

By 1982 Marines on peacekeeping missions wore an embroidered American flag on the upper left sleeve for overseas deployments, a practice similar to aviation units which wore flags on the flight-suit. The reconnaissance units adopted this, with the use of velcro backing for instant removal or application depending on the situation. In 1991, after some years of discussion, cloth name tapes were authorized similar to those of the Army and Air Force. These were in black letters on green webbing for woodland utilities, and brown letters on tan webbing for desert utilities: 'U.S. Marines' over the left chest pocket, and the individual's last name over the right chest pocket of the utility jacket.

During World War Two, plain metal identity discs ('dog tags') engraved with name, religion, blood type, service number and status were issued in pairs and worn on neck cords or chains. In case of death one was taken for reporting and the other was left with the body for identification by graves registration units. By the Korean War identification tags were

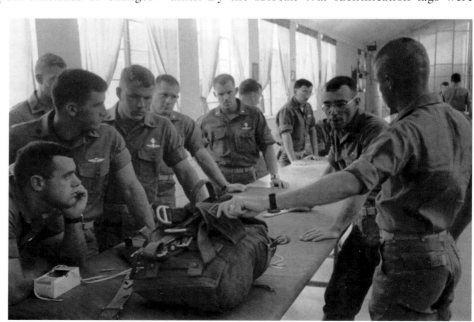

Apart from South-East Asian deployments, recon units had other commitments to support NATO, SEATO, and inter-American defence agreements. These FMF Atlantic Marines are instructed in the T10 parachute as part of a 1974 jumpmaster course for reconnaissance unit leaders. Note the insignia placement on M62 utilities, the standard field uniform throughout the 1970s. The olive green undershirt was a local affectation. (Coulter)

rectangular aluminium tags with an individual's name, service number or social security number, religion and blood type. Also issued in pairs, they were worn around the neck on a chain or attached to the laces of boots. Depending on the assignment, a Recon Marine could carry his identification card and tags, or leave them – and any other distinguishing material – behind to frustrate enemy intelligence in case of death or capture. Tape or rubber sheaths were used to silence the tags from jingling.

Headwear

Various headwear was available for recon when World War Two began, including khaki or sage green overseas caps, the sage green 'Daisy May' M36 utility hat, the khaki tropical sun helmet, a black rubberized fabric rain hat, and even the felt campaign hat. In 1943 the distinctive sage green herringbone utility 'cover' was introduced and became the common headwear, with and without the M1 helmet. This M43 cap was modified in the M44 version, which had a slightly more pronounced bill and a black printed eagle, globe and anchor printed on the front. Rank insignia could be fixed at the crown when not visible elsewhere. An attempt to mandate this in the 1980s met with resistance, and it remains an individual practice. When not in use the utility cover was folded and kept in the helmet liner. This cap was subsequently issued in herringbone material as the M56, and in olive green sateen as the M58; it was issued in ERDL[3] camouflage in 1978, and woodland camouflage from 1982. A utility cover existed in desert camouflage, but was generally replaced by the desert hat.

During the Vietnam era tropical ('boonie' or 'bush') hats of all types were available in olive green and in camouflage patterns. Versions were manufactured with the various hot weather uniforms, as the hat fully covered the head and neck. Issued to ground reconnaissance units and purchased or traded on the local economy, they became a distinctive recon item worn in lieu of the utility cover. Some degree of modification resulted, including cutting the brim back and adding rank and unit insignia. The number of locally made varieties ensured a degree of individuality similar to that possible by imaginative setting up of a beret.

[3] Engineer Research Development Laboratory.

Detachment equipment on display prior to a six-month deployment to the Mediterranean; this was in addition to the gear issued to individuals. It includes an inflatable boat (IBS), MC1-1 parachutes and equipment bags, rappelling ropes and slings, SCUBA gear, various radios, 'starlight' scope, M60 machine gun, and initial terminal guidance beacons. (USMC)

A recon team being inspected by a sergeant prior to a fleet exercise at Camp Lejeune in 1975. The jungle utilities, boots, and rucksacks reflect South-East Asian experience; these uniforms and equipment were held at unit level for field use and were not available to other Marines, who still wore the sateen utilities and leather combat boots. (USMC)

The possibility of adopting berets had been discussed since World War Two, based in part on admiration of the green berets worn by the British Royal Marine Commandos and copied widely in other countries including the Vietnamese Marine Corps. While popular with some, many Marines considered the beret characteristic of either 'Frenchmen or Girl Scouts', and it never caught on. Sweat rags made from olive green towels or cravat bandages were worn around the neck or head; a sweat band could also be made from the strap and safety pin of the issued cloth ammunition bandoleer. Another enduring recon favourite, and a useful item for cooler climates, is the knitted wool stocking hat or 'watch cap' in navy blue or olive green.

The outbreak of World War Two found the Marines using the M1917 pattern helmet. The M1 'Steel Kelly' helmet with separate fibre liner was adopted in 1941, and in service the following year. This helmet, with single chin strap, was used in World War Two, Korea and Vietnam. With alterations to the chin straps and padding, as the M1C, it was used for parachute jumps. The helmet was issued to all hands, but was only worn by reconnaissance units when absolutely necessary, as opposed to the standard infantry practice of wearing it constantly.

A helmet cover was developed with the camouflage uniforms, in reversible green and brown spotted herringbone material. Two main types evolved, the first in 1943, the other in 1944, the second pattern in a denim cloth with foliage slits. A globe and anchor stencilled emblem was applied to some. In 1962 a Defense Department standard leaf pattern canvas cloth helmet cover was adopted; this had reversible green and brown sides, and was used throughout the Vietnam War. The ERDL pattern non-reversible cover in cotton wind-resistant rip-stop poplin appeared in the 1970s. These covers soon faded with use far beyond that found in Army units. Bands were used to hold foliage in place on the helmets; these were either made of rubber inner tube material or Army issue olive green elastic bands. In reconnaissance units the helmet cover was worn by itself in 'pirate' or 'gypsy' fashion, as a head wrap to avoid the disadvantages of the helmet on patrol while still breaking up the head's distinctive shape.

In 1984 the Personal Armor System Ground Troops (PASGT) helmet was adopted – the 'Fritz' helmet. This was supposed to provide greater protection, stability, and comfort than the M1 helmet and was made in one piece from Kevlar. It was heavier, however, and no longer provided field expedient wash basins or lightweight helmet liners. It was used as a parachute helmet, with modifications to the straps and padding. A cloth helmet cover was issued in single-sided woodland and desert patterns.

Utility Uniforms

Though American combat uniforms appear the same, the knowledgeable observer can detect differences between soldiers, Marines, and Recon Marines. This is due to unique procurement, supply practices, and the local terrain and situation. Factors include individual or unit preference, authorized weapons, unit missions and the type of organization (combat, support, or service). The supply system is not universal enough to allow completely uniform appearance. Marines also have an affection for 'salty' clothing and equipment – they prefer older items to newer issue, in order to convey an image of experience, or the impression that they have been in the field so long that appearance had become secondary to function.

World War Two uniforms developed from the green wool and cotton khaki service uniforms used by Marines at the start of the war. The characteristic dress blues worn on ship and barracks influenced uniform development. Both green and khaki uniforms saw service as combat uniforms, but were unsatisfactory for the demands of the Pacific. According to the Marine Corps Historical Center's material curator Kenneth L. Smith-Christmas, a blue denim fatigue uniform was available for particularly dirty duties. It consisted of a pair of bib-style overalls and a jacket similar to those worn by farmers and mechanics. It was worn with the khaki shirt and field hat or garrison cap. The denim work uniform was subsequently manufactured from a green herringbone material in use when the war began.

In 1941 the M41 utility uniform was adopted; this consisted of a jacket and trousers made of sage green cotton herringbone material. The jacket had two patch pockets on the skirt and a single pocket on the left breast. Its exposed metal buttons were stamped 'U.S. Marine Corps', and it had the distinctive Marine Corps emblem stencilled on the chest pocket. The trousers had two front slash pockets, two rear patch pockets, and metal fly buttons. This became the standard combat uniform of the war years and continued to serve through the 1950s, proving to be hard wearing. It was designed to be worn as an over-garment for the service uniforms and was seen in mixed shirt and cap combinations.

Refinements in the utility uniform came from experience during the Pacific campaigns and the demands of the Parachute and Raider units. An improved utility uniform, the M44, was made in sage green herringbone twill. The jacket was altered, having two large horizontal 'map' pockets in either side of the chest, with buttoned slash openings, and a

Combat swimming required open-circuit diving equipment, here being prepared for a practice dive on a landing craft utility (LCU). Neoprene rubber wet-suits were worn for protection in open water. The SCUBA gear was a commercial type purchased at unit level and modified for military use. (Coulter)

A reason for perfecting diving skills was the use of submarines to put recon teams ashore. The group on the submarine's deck is inspecting the forward escape trunk used to get in and out of the vessel. The Marines are in the informal 'amphib' uniform of swimming shorts and canvas diving shoes with utility shirts. (USMC)

Submarine preparation included rigging ascent and descent lines from the hatch to the conning tower for use by swimmers outside the hull. Weapons, uniforms and equipment were waterproofed, and taken through the hatch or stowed externally. These Marines and sailors wear a safety harness while on deck. (USMC)

flap-covered chest pocket on the left chest bearing the Marine emblem. This jacket was worn loose outside of the trousers. The trousers had two flap-covered leg pockets, and a single large flap-covered pocket across the seat of the trousers. Exposed metal buttons were used on both the jacket and trousers.

By 1943 reconnaissance units were being issued camouflage uniforms. The first pattern (M43) was cut along the same lines as the M41 uniform, using cotton herringbone twill material. It was a reversible four-colour design, with the Army's OQMG[4] spotted motif in a predominantly brown side and a predominantly green side. It used black covered metal snap fasteners instead of buttons. The jacket had a single patch pocket on the right skirt and a patch pocket with an emblem on the left chest; when reversed the two pockets were in the same positions on the opposite side. The trousers had a right-front slash pocket and a left-rear patch pocket, again duplicated on the other side.

A second camouflage uniform was later designed; the M44 was a simplified version of the M43, with two deep horizontal chest pockets and had 'U.S. Marine Corps' metal buttons instead of snaps. The trousers had two front slash pocket openings fastened by snaps – allowing access from either side, a single

[4] Office of the Quartermaster General.

31

covered pocket across the trouser seat and a fly front with metal buttons.

These 'camouflage suits' were issued to regular and special units as supplementary clothing until the end of the war. They were hot, and were subject to extreme fading. Their chief drawback was known as early as 1944, when the Army commented that while the mottled pattern blended with foliage, the lighter colours were 'especially noticeable during movement'; and camouflage clothing alone could not conceal a Marine. Only the camouflage helmet cover, poncho, and shelter-half remained in general use after 1945.

In 1953, during the Korean War, the utility jacket was designated as a shirt by the removal of lower patch pockets from the M41 version; this and the M44 jacket were worn with the jacket/skirt tucked into the trousers. Camouflage clothing remained the province of the Recon Marines, being unit instead of individual clothing. Stocks were maintained throughout the Korean War; but by the time force reconnaissance companies and division reconnaissance battalions were formed in the late

1950s this clothing was being obtained from defence disposal sources as surplus 'rags'. Some World War Two items were found in unit stores as late as 1979.

The Korean War brought the need for supplementary winter clothing. For Marines, even those who had served in Iceland and North China, this was a change from the hot and wet climate of the Pacific. Korean War Marines remember wearing wool service shirts and trousers as undergarments with utility uniforms prior to the issue of cold weather clothing. The M50 and M51 cold weather clothing was designed to be worn in a layered fashion that trapped air between the inner bulk and the water- and windproof shells. Use was first made of wool, down, and cotton poplin; in later years quilted nylon, polyester pile, and Goretex served to update the basic design.

An initial layer consisted of winter undershirt and drawers, an inner layer of wool jacket and trousers and an outer layer of either field jacket and trouser shell (which also came with a liner) or utility uniforms. The M51 hooded parka shell and liner was worn over this combination. A single layer arctic camouflage ('overwhite') trouser and parka were developed to cover the olive green basic uniform in snow conditions. Weapons and web gear were given a disrupted pattern through the generous use of white medical tape. An insulated rubber ('Mickey Mouse') boot was worn; this kept feet warm at the expense of making them sweat with movement, and the need to

Individual equipment, including fighting and subsistence loads, minus rations and ammunition. At the top is the rucksack used exclusively by recon. On a poncho liner, from the upper left, are Nomex flight gloves, nylon 'silent' rifle sling, mixed M56 and LC1 belt and harness with M62 canteens, 'jungle' first aid kit, M42 pouch and compass, poncho, M16 rifle with 30-round magazine, M18 antipersonnel mine, smoke and tear gas grenades, map and notebook, and K-Bar knife with day/ night flare. (USMC)

1: Scout, Division Scout Company, USA, 1942
2: Regimental scout-sniper, South Pacific, 1943
3: Amphibious scout, Corps Recon Bn., Western Pacific, 1945

A

Korea
1: Recon scout, Special Ops. Grp., 1950
2: Regimental scout-sniper, 1951
3: Marine, Division Recon Co., 1953

B

1: Surface combat swimmer, 1954
2: Open-circuit combat swimmer, 1958
3: Amphibious scout, Puerto Rico, 1962

C

1: Free-fall parachutist, 1962
2: Force recon, Vietnam, 1967
3: MACV-PRU advisor, Vietnam, 1969

D

1: Division recon, Vietnam, 1970
2: Static-line parachute pathfinder, Panama, 1974
3: Static-line parachutist, Arizona, 1975

E

1: Recon scout, NATO Northern Flank, 1976
2: Open-circuit combat swimmer, Caribbean, 1978
3: Physical training uniform, California, 1981

F

1: Recon scout, SEATO, 1981
2: Free-fall parachutist, DAT, 1988
3: Closed-circuit combat swimmer, Mediterranean, 1988

G

1: Recon scout-sniper, North Carolina, 1990
2: Direct Action Team, Liberia, 1990
3: Recon scout, Persian Gulf, 1990

H

1: Service dress uniform, 1970s
2: Utility uniform, 1980s
3: Utility uniform, 1990s

3

2

1

I

Shoulder insignia, 1945; see text commentary for detailed caption

J

1a

1b

1c

2d

1a-c: Recon breast insignia; see text commentary for detailed caption
2a-d: Informal force recon insignia; see text commentary for detailed caption

2a

2c

2b

Informal division recon insignia; see text commentary for detailed caption

L

replace socks at frequent intervals. These were at first made in black, and later white, rubber. The M51 cold weather clothing remained standard, with some minimal improvements, until the mid-1970s, when experience in NATO showed the need for an updated design. The extended cold weather clothing system (ECWCS) is one result of this effort, although this is itself based on the layering principle.

After Korea the M56 sage green herringbone utility shirt was adopted; this had two patch chest pockets with flaps, a single map pocket, and covered plastic buttons. It was followed by the M58 pattern, of the same design in olive green sateen cloth. Both the M56 and M58 had a stencilled branch-of-service emblem on the left breast pocket. A common Department of Defense procurement system subsequently went into effect, resulting in uniform changes originating outside the Marine Corps. Adopted in 1962, in common with the other services, were cotton olive green (OG 107) sateen utilities, black combat boots, and the leaf pattern helmet cover and shelter-half. The shirt had two flap-covered patch chest pockets; the trousers, two front slash opening patch pockets

Operations were by four-man recon teams, usually with an extra communicator and a Navy corpsman – a total of six personnel. This 1976 patrol have rigger-taped M16 rifles, PRC75 and 77 radios, M65 field jackets with camouflage utilities, and use mixed M56 and LC1 & 2 individual equipment. After years in tropical climates, dismounted tracking and border control operations were conducted in the deserts of Arizona and California. (USMC)

and two covered seat pockets. Green plastic buttons were used. The material was not as durable as herringbone fabric; it retained heat in hot weather, and did not dry out easily in the wet. Even so, this simple sateen uniform – with minor modifications over time – remained the utility outfit for two decades.

When the Vietnam War expanded in 1965, Marine Recon units had few options in field clothing. The M62 utility uniform proved unsatisfactory and a variety of expedients were tried, including commercial 'duck hunter' and Vietnamese camouflage materials. Three official shirt, jacket, and trouser utility uniform combinations were used by Recon Marines during the war. They were, in sequence: from 1965, sateen utilities; from 1966, jungle utilities; and from

1968, camouflage utilities. The jungle and camouflage utilities were supplementary clothing designed for use in Vietnam and were of a light, strong, quick-drying cloth. Olive green and camouflaged utilities were worn as issued in service, though these were generally issued later to Marine than to Army units. As the war progressed and Army items were relied upon, Marines began to look increasingly like soldiers and, eventually, the camouflage uniform was adapted as a distinct issue to all in the III Marine Amphibious Force.

The first pattern jungle utilities were designed for the Special Forces, based on World War Two Army Airborne clothing; they were an olive green colour, in wind-resistant rip-stop cotton poplin (OG107, Type 1). The jacket had four pleated bellows pockets and was worn outside the trousers. The trousers had four pockets on the hips and two expanding cargo pockets on the legs. Buttons were plastic and allowed closure at the collar and wrist, the trouser legs were held in place by tie-downs. The uniform was durable and fast-drying. Although sev-

eral modifications evolved, the basic design remained the same.

A camouflage version of the jungle utilities was first used in 1967, in the four-colour ERDL leaf pattern requested by special operations personnel. The jacket and trousers were of camouflage, 100% cotton wind-resistant rip-stop poplin (Class 2). Popular with recon units, it suffered the problem of most camouflage uniforms: it was great while standing still, but drew attention when moving. Over the years modifications in material, pocket design, and shoulder straps and waist tabs were made.

Other items developed by ARPA[5] during the Vietnam War for small independent action forces which found use in Marine Recon units included a jungle pack and rucksack, two-quart canteen, jungle hammock, lightweight knitted shirt (sleeping shirt), wet weather parka and coveralls (rain suit), and lightweight poncho. The utilities and boots developed were so successful that they became standard items after the war.

[5] US Army Advance Research Projects Agency.

In the early 1970s a distinctive and unofficial mode of dress was common among reconnaissance personnel. This consisted of sateen utility uniforms and breast insignia worn with olive green undershirts and Corcoran jump boots. Jungle and camouflage clothing was used in various reconnaissance units for operations and training long after Vietnam, continuing a pattern of wear that eventually found its way into general service. Camouflage utilities in 100% cotton rip-stop poplin replaced the sateen uniform throughout the Corps in 1978, and were worn with slight tailoring modifications which simplified manufacture. Their quick-drying qualities, light weight and wind resistance were as valued by infantry as by recon units for desert, temperate and cold climates.

In 1982 the woodland pattern battle dress uniform (BDU) was adopted. This was similar in design to the previous jungle and camouflage utilities, with simpler pockets, in a 50% cotton and 50% nylon blend. The combat coat and trousers were treated to present less infrared signature and allowed for more temperate wear; but they were criticized for retaining heat and moisture, particularly after the Grenada and Panama operations. Subsequently a light-weight version was made, using 100% cotton rip-stop material.

The desert camouflage worn in the Gulf War was developed at the same time as supplementary clothing to meet the need for hot weather clothing in dry climates. The desert pattern camouflage utilities were 50% cotton and 50% nylon, in a six-colour design ('chocolate chip'). During the Gulf War a second pattern was fielded in three colours, and modifications were made to simplify manufacture. Additional items used included the night desert uniform, a parka and trousers in a desert green grid pattern that enhanced protection from night vision devices.

Shirt and jacket sleeves were worn rolled up or down, depending on the weather and tactical situation. For a time in Vietnam, sleeves were allowed to be cut off, and were either left frayed or hemmed. In the field, the herringbone and sateen 'shirt' was worn outside of the trouser waist to circulate air; at times the various jackets have been worn tucked in, for example during parachuting or rappelling.

The issue khaki web belt with open face brass

Left: Another method to deliver swimmers was by high speed cast and recovery, developed in World War Two. A landing craft towed a rubber boat alongside, which served as a platform to drop a line of swimmers off the beach. At Guantanamo Bay, Cuba, an amphibious scout is recovered using a sling; this is caught, swinging him up onto the rubber boat, and then into the landing craft. (Coulter)

Right: Rubber boats have been a mainstay of amphibious recon from the beginning, and several generations of inflatables evolved with varying degrees of success. This 1st Reconnaissance Battalion boat crew conduct a surf passage in California in 1982, using a military amphibious reconnaissance system (MARS) boat with rigid keel (USMC)

buckle was in use from World War Two onwards. Worn with all uniforms, the web belt remained popular as one of the few unique Marine Corps items, even though subdued colours were more practical; some of the wartime versions had a darker colour khaki and subdued brass. It could also double as a cargo strap to secure ammunition boxes, sleeping bags, etc. Supplemental belts were used, such as 'jungle' belts made from suspender straps, parachute harness webbing, and even captured enemy belts.

White underwear was used until locally dyed or manufactured olive green items were available; olive green items were used around 1944 and 1966. Often no underwear was worn for comfort in humid conditions. Sometimes seen in South-East Asia were Special Service[6]-funded olive green undershirts and sweat shirts, with wing or division names printed over 'Vietnam' on the front in black, block letters. As pioneered by Recon Marines, the green undershirt became a general purpose item by 1978 for wear with camouflage utilities, followed in 1982 by the Army's brown undershirt when stocks became available.

Footwear

World War Two and Korean War footwear consisted of a 'field service shoe' – an ankle boot with tan leather rough-out uppers and a black cord and rubber sole. These 'boondockers' were worn with khaki canvas leggings to confine the trouser legs. The M34

[6] This was a welfare and recreation agency.

version was of three-piece construction with a web canvas instep strap; the Marine leggings had six hooks and eyelets, the Army's had nine. Later in the war leggings were dispensed with, or worn over the shoes and under the trousers to keep dirt out of the field shoes while leaving the trousers loose for ventilation and drainage. For water work or creeping, government canvas shoes with rubber soles were available, as were commercial athletic and basketball shoes. Then, as now, their long term use was avoided because of their lack of durability and protection.

Field shoes and leggings were still used in Korea in 1950, but were phased out before the war's end. Combat boots were introduced when Army M43 leather combat boots were worn, a unique Marine Corps rough-out version with hook and eye closures was also issued. Trousers were worn bloused around the boot top with 'blousing garters' rather than tucked into the boot in Army style. In 1962 the Marines adopted all-black leather equipment; leather gear not issued in black had to be stained and polished. At this time Defense Department common combat boots were introduced. Various comments have been made over the years that these boots were too heavy for water work, too hot for jungle work and not thick enough for mountain or cold weather wear. Recent innovations include speed-lacing loops, suede finish, and the Panama sole as used on the jungle boot.

In Vietnam green nylon and black leather tropi-

Clandestine observation and reporting was the primary job of recon patrols before and after amphibious landings. A corporal team-leader reports an enemy sighting using the PRC77 radio carried in a tropical rucksack; the communicator and scout provide local security. They use jungle utilities and M56 and LC1 & 2 gear. (USMC)

cal combat boots 'jungle boots' were preferred and worn as available, again later than in Army units. They remained a popular item for field wear into the 1980s and were standard issue from 1989 – another example of a recon style becoming generally accepted. In 1990 a khaki nylon and tan leather desert boot was issued during the Gulf War, the so-called 'Schwarzkopf boot'.

White, black and olive green socks were worn in all-cotton, all-wool and blends with nylon. In the field, a spare pair was kept in a plastic radio-battery bag to rotate when the worn pair was wet. Boot socks were used in recon to pad or silence other items of equipment and were also tied to the pack and used to carry ration cans.

Supplementary Clothing

A variety of supplementary clothing, including most of the camouflage uniforms discussed, has long existed for use by Marines in general and Recon Marines in particular. A characteristic of these items is that they are normally held by the unit or command and issued as needed. Most were developed as special theatre requirements for environmental changes, and have continued to fill these needs. Some items have become so common as to be virtually standard, including the field jacket, raincoat and various other waterproof clothes. Supplementary uniform items allow for a certain amount of mixing and matching, much of which does not comply with approved codes – giving rise to comments about 'raggedy-ass Marines'. It should be kept in mind that once overseas the Marines were far from their depots in the United States, and had a tradition of adapting any available material.

Frequently worn, to the point of being characteristic, recon physical training uniform (PT gear) is distinctly individual and is the only attire that allows a degree of elaboration with name tags and informal insignia. PT gear includes issue olive green (PT shorts) or khaki swim trunks (UDT shorts). These shorts are worn with a utility cover, shirt, combat boots or coral shoes ('pixie boots') as an 'amphib' uniform for water work.

The need for something warm to wear in the field rather than a jacket has been a constant problem, even in 'sunny tropic scenes'. This need has been met with wool uniform shirts, sweat shirts, warm-up

A bridge reconnaissance conducted at night in North Carolina by a recon platoon as part of its evaluation and indoctrination. They wear M62 utilities and mixed M56 and LC2 webbing.

Exercise targets were selected to take teams into civilian areas, where local authorities were warned to look out for them and report them. (Coulter)

jerseys and sweaters worn under the utility uniform. Some of these were issue items and others were from commercial sources in a variety of colours. A Marine commander at Khe Sanh recalled that wool shirts were issued to his unit during the 'winter' monsoon period of 1967–68. The dark green shirt was the Marine Corps uniform item of cold weather clothing, serving the same purpose as the Army polyester knitted 'sleeping shirt'. The theory was that these could be kept dry in the pack during the day, then used at night in place of a wet utility shirt. In practice, they were worn under the utility jacket in cold or wet weather and there are photographs of them serving as an outer garment. One recon practice

Small arms, demolitions, and supporting arms have all been used for both ambushes and defence. The balance between combat and stealth involves constantly changing choices depending on the mission and circumstances. A

'Claymore' anti-personnel mine is installed on a trail by two jungle utility-clad Marines, one covering the other. The command-detonated mine is useful for surprise, and for flank and rear protection. (USMC)

jackets were available during cold weather, in some cases from unit stocks or as replacements from Okinawa. A field jacket in woodland ERDL camouflage pattern with a skirt long enough to cover the utility jacket was adopted in 1983, but took some time to get into general use.

Rubberized fabric foul-weather suits and raincoats were also available. The World War Two variety were black or green. Rain suits were issued to armour and motor transport crews and adopted by recon teams, who found the poncho impractical for patrol. Vietnam-issue parkas and coveralls were of olive green rubberized fabric that darkened in colour when wet. Korean, Okinawan, or Vietnamese-made items weighed less and could be in any colour, though usually green or camouflage. During the war velcro closures were added to the rain suits and field jackets without a change to the model designation. Recent innovations include the use of Goretex for parkas and trousers in the woodland camouflage pattern.

Individual & Unit Equipment

A Recon Marine, on an amphibious assault for reconnaissance-in-force or raid operations, could find himself dressed, armed and equipped with as much gear as an infantryman. He could alternatively have nothing more than swimming trunks, a knife and a pistol for a beach reconnaissance prior to a landing – a wide range of possibilities. Equipment for specialized tasks added to the basic load carried and caused hard choices between comfort and function. 'High-speed gear', unit equipment for mission-essential tasks, included communications, optics, amphibious, airborne, demolition and chemical defence items. Each unit had access to special equipment, which often ended up being used for more mundane chores and identified Recon Marines in a unique way.

The Marine Corps classified web gear as basic individual equipment, supplementary individual equipment, and organizational individual equipment. Known as '782' gear, M1941 individual combat equipment served in World War Two, Korea and South-East Asia. It was modified with M1961 belts and pouches. In Vietnam, M1956 load-carrying equipment (LCE) in olive green cotton canvas was made available, as well as M1967 modernized load-carrying equipment (MLCE and LC1) in olive green

was to use the field jacket's insulated liner worn under the utility jacket for less bulk and weight. In 1978 the wool service sweater was adopted. This olive green pullover with shoulder and elbow patches was a version of the Royal Marines 'woolly pully'.

The field jacket was designed as an outer garment for temperate and cold weather. In World War Two the Army's khaki M41 field jacket was used, and also worn with service uniforms overseas. By 1945 it was seen with cloth rank and unit insignia, a departure from normal field wear. In Korea the olive green M43 and M51 field jackets and liners were issued. Both were of a four-pocket 'bush' jacket design, and were worn with a liner, hood, scarf and gloves to increase warmth. In Vietnam the M51 and M65 field

nylon. All purpose lightweight individual carrying equipment (ALICE or LC2) in olive green nylon entered the Fleet Marine Force around 1974. The more recent direct action tasks have required the acquisition of specialized equipment – 'black gear' – from commercial sources supplying police-style special weapons and equipment.

Over the years the 'fighting load' has consisted of a belt, braces, canteen, first aid pouch, ammunition pouches, and entrenching tools (shovel, pick, machete). A 'subsistence load' was carried in the light marching or ALICE pack, and included rations, spare clothing, poncho, shelter-half, and blanket or sleeping bag. Despite a desired body-to-load weight ratio of three to one, the typical reconnaissance man carried much more than the theoretical 50 pound maximum – averages were more like 80 to 100 pounds. This was encouraged by the limitations of helicopter and vehicle transport once a unit was on foot. The ALICE field pack and frame allowed for more to be carried, a benefit to recon if not to the infantry.

The use of body armour by reconnaissance personnel varied with the task at hand; it was issued on the same scale as to infantry units. In recent years the use of issue or special-purpose armour by hostage recovery teams has been an option. Modern body armour was introduced to Marines in Korea with the M51 and M55 protective body armour, the 'Flak'

A job nobody wanted – nuclear, chemical, and biological survey work. This required the use of M17A1 masks and protective clothing, making patrolling as strenuous as underwater work, with a consequent reduction of performance. At the Pickle Meadow mountain training centre, two recon team members show the front and rear of full protective clothing worn with LC2 and ALICE equipment.

Current inflatables include the rigid-hull Avon Searider with twin outboard motors and a cockpit comparable to the rigid raider craft. This allows long distance, high speed expeditions carrying a realistic load of Marines and equipment; it also serves as a 'mother' boat for smaller craft or swimmers.

Marine Recon jumped from helicopters in training and used fixed-wing aircraft for operations, the KC-130 Hercules being the most sophisticated 'transport' in the Marine Corps inventory. This accommodates up to 90 paratroopers; recon teams used fewer jumpers, leaving space for additional fuel and equipment. (Lockheed)

jacket, with its angular plates. The Kevlar PASGT Body Armour was in use from 1982, in a woodland camouflage pattern, or with a desert-pattern cover.

Field modifications included taped or rubber-cushioned identification tags; metal canteens covered with boot socks to prevent noise; and yards of black electrical or green 'rigger's' tape to cushion, fasten, or cover equipment. Force recon's parachute riggers manufactured or modified equipment to mission and individual standards. Black and green spray paint or camouflage grease-paint toned down both skin and equipment.

Recon travelled 'as lightly as possible', but had to fight in varied situations. A 1944 manual stated that the patrols should be armed with 'weapons which can be conveniently and silently handled, and which can develop a large volume of fire'. Service rifles, shotguns, sub-machine guns and pistols were judged 'excellent' patrol weapons. Rifles and other weapons came with individual accessories: sling, bayonet, and cleaning kit. Various silencers and sights have been tried, although none has really stood out. Special circumstances called for grenades, anti-tank weapons, light machine guns and light mortars. The selection of small arms depended upon the mission and the proficiency of the patrol members, and the 'choice of silent weapons may be left to individuals'. Bayonets, knives, blackjacks, machetes, axes and strangling cords were essential for silence behind enemy lines.

For an amphibious patrol of less than a day's duration, the scouts at Tarawa carried M1 rifles, 'a hunting knife, an appropriate amount of ammunition, and two hand grenades'. In Vietnam a division recon platoon leader listed his load as 'four grenades, a poncho, a pop-up flare, two illumination grenades, a stick of grease paint, toilet paper, mosquito repellent, a P-38 can opener attached to a shoelace tied to the pack frame, three large compress bandages, and a toothbrush for cleaning my rifle', along with water, rations, and ammunition. According to a force recon medical corpsman, other preparations included not bathing or shaving the day prior to a patrol, wearing utilities washed without soap and air dried, and assembling 'a comfortable and practical fighting uniform and rig'.

References

Official Volumes, *History of US Marine Corps Operations in World War II, US Marine Operations in Korea, US Marines in Vietnam, Marines in the Persian Gulf* (Headquarters, 1954–93).

Kevin Lyles, *Vietnam: US Uniforms in Colour Photographs* (Windrow & Greene, 1992).

Jim Moran, *US Marine Corps Uniforms & Equipment in World War 2* (Windrow & Greene, 1992).

B.H. Norton, *Force Recon Diary, 1969* (Ivy, 1991).

P.R. Senich, *US Marine Scout-Sniper* (Paladin, 1993).

P.R. Young, *First Recon – Second to None* (Ivy, 1992).

THE PLATES

A1: Division Scout Company, United States, 1942

At the start of World War Two the M41 utility uniform showed a pragmatic starkness, with its only adornments the stencilled service insignia on the chest pocket and the stamped metal buttons. This scout is wearing the newly issued M1 steel helmet and an M37 automatic rifleman's cartridge belt. He is armed with the dependable M1918 Browning Automatic Rifle, the 'BAR'.

A2: Regimental scout-sniper, South Pacific, 1943

A sniper in khaki shirt and utility trousers which need camouflaging. His weapon is the M1903 Springfield rifle with telescopic sight, favoured for precision shooting, and he wears the M36 pistol belt and M10 canteen. In the Pacific the khaki tropical uniform was, for the most part, worn only by Marines in rear areas or on board ship. At times it was mixed with the utility uniform which had been intended to be worn over tropical or temperate service uniforms.

A3: Corps Reconnaissance Battalion, Western Pacific, 1945

This amphibious scout wears his helmet cover as headgear, and the camouflage uniform for a beach reconnaissance. He uses a sling-line to bring M1 Garand rifles through a standard 25in. submarine hatch. He wears the improved M23 cartridge belt, an M42 first aid case, and a canteen on the opposite hip. The distinctive Marine M43 camouflage utilities were used by various combat units, but became associated with paratroopers, Raiders, snipers, and recon. For a number of reasons they were impractical for general use, although the helmet cover became a distinctive Marine Corps item.

B1: Special Operations Group, Korea, 1950

Reflecting the mixed-service nature of the group, gear came from Army, Navy and Marine sources. Dress and equipment was designed for raids and demolitions rather than reconnaissance and surveillance. This recon scout wears M44 utilities, a navy

Airborne methods have also been perfected using different aircraft. Rappelling from a hovering helicopter allows rapid exit without landing, as practised here by an 'indoctrination' platoon member; he exits a CH-46 on a 120-foot nylon rope passing through a metal snap-link attached to his seat harness, controlling descent by hand, wearing heavy leather gloves. The M62 utilities indicate training rather than operations. (Coulter)

wool 'watch' cap, modified gloves, a toggle-rope with leather work gloves, a cartridge belt with K-Bar knife, compass and M38 wire cutter, and leggings with field shoes. His weapon is the M1 service rifle.

B2: Regimental scout-sniper, Korea, 1951

Snipers were organized and trained in Korea at division level. This was possible due to the availability of World War Two veterans and equipment. This Marine displays an M1903 Springfield rifle with Unertl telescopic sight and carries ammunition in a bandoleer. His dress is informal, consisting of an M1 helmet, Army field sweater, M41 utility trousers and field shoes. The M3 fighting and utility knife and the Mk2 grenade are an incongruous touch.

B3: Division Reconnaissance Company, Korea, 1953

The Korean War was fought using World War Two era equipment, in this case the M44 camouflage utilities worn almost exclusively by recon units. The Marine depicted is moving into position after leaving a helicopter on a hilltop. He displays the brown side of the reversible uniform, although his helmet cover shows the green side, with rank chevrons inked by hand on both sleeves. He carries an M1 rifle, M41 pack with M43 entrenching tool, cartridge belt and canteen. The belt carries eight-round clips in each of its ten pockets.

Advanced unit qualifications focused on getting to and from hostile areas. Marines specialized in working with the US Navy; here a force recon platoon prepares to board patrol boats on North Carolina's Inland Waterway for a riverine exercise. They wear M62 utilities, leather combat boots, UDT life vests, and knife belts.

C1: Surface combat swimmer, 1954

Amphibious patrols used small craft and surface swimming to get to the beach. Protective clothing – including exposure suits – were adopted; these took into account various water temperatures. This amphibious scout wears the basic equipment needed to get ashore, including a dry suit, face mask, and swim fins. At his waist is a pistol belt which holds a K-Bar knife and little else. When going further than the beach a waterproof bag would be used to carry uniform and weapons.

C2: Open-circuit combat swimmer, 1958

Open-circuit diving technology developed with other insertion techniques. The Marines added their own tactical considerations to what the Navy was doing, to make a combat swimmer out of a 2d Class Diver (SCUBA). Marine reconnaissance units adopted underwater swimming as an aid to the use of submarines, and free ascent as a method of 'clandestine insertion' which did not require the submarine to surface. Equipment was obtained from naval and commercial sources; this Marine diver 'suits up' with double tanks, twin-hose regulator, cartridge belt with lead weights, instruments, and swim fins. A slate for recording hydrographic information and a face mask complete the outfit.

C3: Amphibious scout, Puerto Rico, 1962

Whether coming ashore on the surface or underwa-

ter, the job dictated which clothing and equipment were selected. In most cases the Marines either remained on the beach or continued ashore beyond the high water point. This required field uniforms and equipment to be carried and put on once a safe position had been reached. This Marine peels off a neoprene wet suit worn with trunks and fins to swim ashore. He is equipped with the M3 sub-machine gun; a 'war belt' and utilities are in the waterproof bag.

D1: Free fall parachutist, 1962

Along with underwater swimming, the use of parachutes to enter enemy territory was developed by Marines to provide a full range of options for reconnaissance units. This development included pioneering efforts in military free fall, allowing high speed and high altitude aircraft to be used. A rigger models the modified T10 parachute used for this; he has a parachute kit-bag under the left main lift webbing. He wears the M58 pattern sateen utility uniform used in garrison, with unofficial Corcoran jump boots. The use of motorcycle or football helmets was typical of Marine Recon, who hid their jump kit after landing.

D2: Force recon, Vietnam, 1967

The standard sateen utility uniform proved inadequate in Vietnam. Reconnaissance units tried a number of innovations from government and commercial sources before the lightweight jungle utilities arrived in sufficient quantities. This Marine wears the first pattern, characterized by the exposed buttons; he also wears the initial pattern jungle boot. His weapon is the M14 service rifle, but his personal equipment reflects a common mix of M41, M61, and M56 patterns (the magazine pouches and K-Bar knife were peculiar to the Marines). The lack of body armour and the use of the bush hat reflect the patrol mission, and the lack of camouflage and pack indicate that this is a rehearsal or inspection. (After Kevin Lyles)

D3: MACV-PRU adviser, Vietnam, 1969

Marines served outside division and force reconnaissance units with the Vietnamese Marine Corps and MACV special operations forces; they were selected for secondment based on their parachute and dive training and previous tours in combat. This enlisted

Additional exercises stressed various cross-country movement methods. In the Sierra Nevada, a mountain leader demonstrates cliff assault techniques to be used by recon patrols serving as guides for other units; note specialized climbing helmets and boots worn with camouflage utilities. The instructor on the left carries an M62 canteen and a sling-rope hung by a snap-link on his belt.

adviser is with a provincial reconnaissance unit – PRU – the action arm of the Phoenix Program to eliminate Communist cadres in South Vietnam. His uniform and equipment reflect this unconventional role: black-dyed 'tiger stripe' uniform, M56 webbing, and the then-scarce CAR15. He carries a PRC25 radio, and holds a bandanna made from a cravat bandage, while controlling a helicopter extraction .

E1: Division recon, Vietnam, 1970

Uniforms and equipment for recon units were tailored to the task at hand. Improvements resulted from experience, increased funding and availability in Vietnam. This Marine wears the preferred ERDL

Parachutes continued to be a force recon speciality, limited to static line methods throughout the 1970s. A recon team exits from the ramp of a CH-53 Sea Stallion at 1,500 feet above the pines of Camp Lejeune. Most Marine Corps drop zones were considered diminutive by the other services. (Coulter)

camouflage utility uniform with jungle boots that were issue throughout the III Marine Amphibious Force by this date. The jungle hat was made from the same pattern material. The pack is a so-called 'ARVN rucksack' designed for the Vietnamese, but superior to the Marine Corps M41 pack and its US Army equivalent. On each side of the pack are special two-quart canteens. He carries the M16 rifle with 20-round magazine, adopted for use during the war. (After Kevin Lyles)

E2: Static line parachute pathfinder, Panama, 1974

After Vietnam, reconnaissance units conducted training deployments with a mix of old and new uniforms and equipment that reflected budget constraints and expanding security responsibilities. This force recon Marine is being inspected prior to a pathfinder mission requiring a parachute jump from a C-130 onto the Gatun Drop Zone. He wears the M62 sateen utilities and full leather combat boots; his helmet is a personally procured motorcycle type. Note the T10 static line parachute and CWIE bag with lowering lines (around a hundred pounds of gear). He carries an M16 rifle on his left side. With the exception of the rifle, little had changed over the previous ten years.

E3: Static line parachutist, rough terrain, Arizona, 1975

Rough terrain suits and tree-jumping techniques were developed by the US Forest Service 'smoke jumpers', used by the British in Malaya, and adopted by the US Army in Korea and Vietnam. The Marines took advantage of this kit to land in areas where there were no drop zones. The jumper wore a specially padded coverall and a helmet with face mask, and carried a rappelling rope in a leg pocket. The object was to snag the parachute in a tree and then lower himself to the ground. This suit was also worn for jumps in rocky terrain. Jumpers used the improved MC1-1 parachute and harness with individual quick release snaps on the chest and leg straps.

F1: Recon scout, NATO, 1976

With increased focus on Europe's northern and southern flank, interest in the conduct of cold weather patrols revived the use, and led to the improvement, of Marine Corps 1950-era clothing and equipment. The older equipment was cumbersome, and the addition of individual and team equipment created sometimes immovable burdens. As a result a new generation of Marines were required for reconnaissance in this new environment. This Recon Marine wears the standard extreme cold weather outfit, including a wool watch cap, arctic camouflage, parka and hood, wool shirt, and insulated boots. His M16 rifle and nylon ALICE load carrying equipment are camouflaged with white medical tape.

F2: Open-circuit combat swimmer, Caribbean, 1978

A Marine listens to last minute instructions before making an off-shore penetration. He wears camouflage utilities instead of a wet suit, and has his rifle fastened to his right shoulder. He uses an improved UDT life preserver and 'Rocket' fins. Underwater swimming techniques had progressed, but were still

A sergeant approaches the ground in the approved 'feet-and-knees together' position; he controls a T10 canopy with toggles affecting direction and descent. A characteristic black motorcycle helmet is used for head protection. He has the M41 haversack under the reserve, and wears his webbing and weapon underneath the parachute harness rather than using an equipment bag and lowering line. (Coulter)

limited by open-circuit equipment despite advances in closed-circuit diving. Emphasis was placed on getting into or out of an enemy area rather than on underwater missions as such. US Army Special Forces programmes provided new ideas, as did the US Navy SEALs; these were adapted to fit the Marine Recon mission.

F3: Physical training uniform, California, 1981

A wide variety of workout clothing existed, subject to unit whims rather than regulation. Issue items such as the khaki swimming trunks or 'UDT' shorts, worn here in division recon, provided some uniformity. Olive green swimming trunks were available, and custom-made varieties existed in camouflage patterns. Undershirts with silk-screened battalion insignia were purchased rather than issued.

G1: Recon scout, SEATO, 1981
This force recon Marine carries a 9mm MP5 submachine gun with silencer. His personal equipment is the nylon LC2 variety with an ALICE pack. He wears the jungle hat associated with the hot-weather uniform, and gloves to protect his hands from thorns and vines. Camouflage utilities were now standard field uniform for all Marines, reflecting a defence build-up in the decade after Vietnam. New weapons and equipment were provided as amphibious, motorized and direct action tasks were assigned.

G2: Free fall parachutist, Direct Action Team, 1988
Military free fall parachute jumping and counter-terrorist missions were assigned at about the same time; a force recon Marine displays the equipment needed for this mix. His leather jump helmet holds an oxygen mask in place, attached to a 'bail out' bottle. He wears the woodland camouflage utilities, flight gloves, '782 gear' under the MT1X parachute harness, with an M17 protective mask on his left hip, and his pack between his thighs. The weapon is the MP5 sub-machine gun for close-quarter combat during hostage rescue.

G3: Closed-circuit combat swimmer, Mediterranean, 1988
Recon diving capabilities were improved with the acquisition of state-of-the-art breathing equipment, such as the Draeger LAR5 apparatus, worn here with a Viking combat diver's suit. The suit allowed for a greater range of water temperature and the smooth rubber exterior reduced drag, even with utilities worn under the suit. The swimmer carries an exposed M16A2, and a waterproof bag for equipment and supplies, reflecting the amphibious nature of his tasks. This gear is a long way from the 'WP' bag and 'Grease Gun' era.

H1: Recon scout-sniper, North Carolina, 1990
The Marine Corps scout-sniper school at Quantico, Virginia, produced the weapons and training needed for an effective 'peacetime' sniping programme. This division recon Marine wears the characteristic 'ghillie' suit to provide concealment for creeping and hiding; it is made from sewing frayed burlap garnish to a woodland utility uniform, and has been given anti-infra-red treatment. His rifle is the improved bolt-action M40 with an M10 Unertl 3×9 power scope.

Training to combine all necessary skills was conducted, with manoeuvres under demanding terrain conditions: amphibious, mountain, arctic, desert, and jungle. A 2d Marine

Division recon company in rubber boats co-operates with an OV-10 Bronco observation aircraft during a patrol of the Cape Fear River. (USMC)

H2: Direct Action Team, Liberia, 1990

Recon Marines mission contingencies include protection or evacuation of diplomatic personnel. This man is dressed and equipped for action during Operation 'Sharp Edge' in Liberia. He wears a low-visibility 'ninja suit', a Goretex coverall normally used for free fall parachute jumping. His personal equipment is commercial black nylon Cordura webbing, with a custom .45 automatic pistol in an 'SAS' style holster for close-quarter combat. Hanging off the 'assault' pack is a standard M17 protective mask. Flame-retardant hood and gloves, elbow and knee pads, goggles, and a light helmet were also used.

H3: Recon scout, Persian Gulf, 1990

This recon scout exhibits the uniform and equipment worn by force and division units during operation 'Desert Shield' and 'Desert Storm'. The desert pattern utilities were a companion design to the woodland uniform, and were put to use on a large scale with the deployment to the Persian Gulf. The so-called 'chocolate chip' scheme was later replaced by a more subdued pattern. His 'boonie' hat is of the same material, with a head-mounted PVS7 night vision device. He carries an ALICE pack with PRC77 radio, two-quart canteen, M17 mask, and LC2 webbing. His rifle is the M16A2 with silent sling and Aimpoint sight. (After Cpl. Richard M. Fitzpatrick)

I1: Service dress uniform, 1970s

A service uniform was worn on more formal occasions, as in this case while graduating from the Greek parachute school. In the 1970s the wool winter service 'greens' were supplemented by a lightweight polyester 'all-season' uniform worn with a khaki shirt and tie. On the Marine's left breast are the Navy-Marine Corps parachute badge, medal ribbons and rifle qualification badge, and on the right is the Greek parachute insignia (not permitted to be worn by regulation). A shirt sleeve uniform for daytime use consisted of green trousers and khaki shirt. Cap and collar badges indicated the service with black Corps emblems.

I2: Utility uniform, 1980s

The camouflage utility uniform was made standard in 1978 and continues as such. The woodland pattern cap, jacket and trousers, worn with boots and green undershirt, emphasize the Marine Corps' field orientation even in garrison. Both heavy and lightweight materials were developed, and modifications in tailoring existed. Collar pin-on rank insignia are displayed for a noncommissioned officer and the dual-qualification badges of a Recon Marine are on the left chest. A heat transfer service emblem is on the left pocket, but is barely visible on this material. Both full leather and jungle boots are authorized for wear. Although starch and heavy pressing were dis-

Some division recon Marines attended the US Army Airborne School, but most did not jump as a duty. An exception were the deep recon platoons, like this one awaiting developments sitting on parachutes and equipment bags at Camp Pendleton. The M65 field jacket is stencilled 'RECON' to prevent use by other units.

Arctic alternated with desert preparations, reflecting different contingency options facing commands based in the United States. Division recon Marines fire M16 rifles, wearing the M51 cold-weather clothing developed during the Korean War, including parka and insulated boots, which improved with NATO experience. White arctic camouflage was available to disrupt the olive green colour.

couraged so as not to defeat anti–infra–red properties, this custom is still in vogue.

I3: Utility uniform insignia, 1990s

Since 1982 units in multinational operations have worn an embroidered American flag on the upper left sleeve, similar to aviator practice, for the period of the deployment only. Officially and unofficially, both visible name stamps and tags had been used in the past. In 1991, after much discussion, Army-style name tapes were adapted for wear with the utility uniform (black on green for woodland pattern, tan on khaki for desert pattern). The Marine's name is worn over his right pocket and 'U.S. Marine' over the left. This changed the use of the iron-on service emblem on the left pocket to the eagle, globe, and anchor only.

J: Shoulder insignia, 1943–47

The colour schemes used for these insignia reflect the official Marine scarlet and gold, and the national colours of red, white and blue. Early shoulder markings were not to be worn in forward areas where they would be seen by the enemy. All insignia depicted in this plate are based on a

Headquarters Bulletin published on 1 August 1945.

J1: Scout, Recon Company, 1st Marine Division

Formed with the division in March 1941 as part of the 'Old Breed'. In 1943 this emblem became the first shoulder insignia to be adopted by Marines. It incorporates the Southern Cross constellation and 'Guadalcanal' battle honour. The scout and recon companies served in Guadalcanal, New Britain, Peleliu, and Okinawa in World War Two; and the Korean War.

J2: Scout Recon Company, 2d Marine Division

This emblem reflects the division's torch-bearer status as the second senior Marine division. It also displays the Southern Cross from South Pacific campaigns. Scout and recon companies served on Tarawa, Saipan, Tinian.

J3: Scout, Recon Company, 3d Marine Division

The 'caltrop' emblem displayed on this insignia represented the division number and its fighting regiments. Scout and recon companies served on Bougainville, Guam, and Iwo Jima.

J4: Scout, Recon Company, 4th Marine Division
Formed with the division in August 1943. The '4' in the insignia matched the airfield runway layout of the division's first battle on Roi-Namur. Division scout and recon companies served in the Marshalls, Saipan, Tinian, Iwo Jima.

J5: Scout, Recon Company, 5th Marine Division
Formed with the division in January 1944. The division was nicknamed the 'Spearhead'. The recon company served on Iwo Jima, the division's only campaign.

J6: Recon Company, 6th marine Division
Formed with the division in September 1944. The company – made up of a number of experienced units, including the former Raider and Parachute Battalions – served on Okinawa. The significance of these Battalions is reflected in this insignia.

J7 & J8: Amphibious Recon Company, Battalion

Formed in 1943, this recon unit served first under the V Amphibious Corps (**7**) whose emblem contained an amphibian and the stars of a major-general. After the Second World War the unit was transferred to Fleet Marine Force Pacific (**8**).

J9 & J10: Raider and parachute insignia
The official use of shoulder insignia ended in 1947, but Raider (**9**) and Parachute (**10**) motifs continued as the basis for informal insignia.

K1: Recon breast insignia, current
The breast insignia worn by Marines qualified in parachute and dive training are Recon Marine hallmarks. The insignia include the Navy SCUBA Diver badge (**1a**), the Navy-Marine Parachutist badge (**1b**), and the Army Basic parachutist badge (**1c**). Breast

Team leaders being briefed before departing on motorized patrols using M151 jeeps in the Mojave Desert. The 'BDU' utility uniform was designed for woodland foliage rather than the desert, and were worn by all Marines from 1978. Vehicles display the disrupted pattern that replaced solid olive green by 1980.

insignia were in gilt, silver, and anodised metal versions. Full-colour and subdued woven cloth insignia were Army and Navy items not used by Marines.

K2: Informal force recon insignia
At unit level a variety of local emblems have been worn on everything except the uniform.

K2a: 2d Force Recon Company
Formed in June 1958 from the FMF Atlantic amphibious reconnaissance company, it is the longest serving force recon company. Elements served in the Dominican Republic, Nato, Lebanon, the Persian Gulf. It is based at Camp Lejeune, North Carolina.

K2b: 4th Force Recon Company
Formed as a reserve unit. Elements served in the Persian Gulf War. Reserve units have traded off both division and force reconnaissance missions, which explains the use of the division motto in this emblem.

K2c: 3d Force Recon Company
Formed in October 1965 as a reserve unit. From 1966 and 1969 it was an active company in the Vietnam War, elements of the unit also served in the Persian Gulf War.

K2d: 1st Force Recon Company
Formed in June 1957 from the FMF Pacific amphibious reconnaissance company. The company was cadred from 1974 until 1987, although it considers itself the senior force recon unit. It served in the Cuban Crisis, Vietnam and Persian Gulf Wars.

L: Informal division recon insignia
Division recon used variations of the standard division insignia, and the 'Billy Bones' of the Raiders, for emblems found on signs, coffee cups, shirts, etc.

L1: 1st Recon Battalion
Formed in May 1958, the premier recon battalion in the senior division. It served in the Cuban Crisis,

Direct action equipment worn by force recon during a cordon-and-search in Somalia. The facing Marine displays helmet, ballistic glasses, armoured equipment vest and radio arrangements. Just visible on the left is an air panel and assault pack on the back of a vest. The desert camouflage utilities have a removable American flag on the left shoulder. The weapon is an MP5 sub-machine gun, in contrast to the infantryman on the right with standard LC2 issue. (Dawson)

Vietnam, and the Persian Gulf War. It is now at Camp Pendleton, California.

L2: 2d Recon Battalion
Formed in January 1958, it served in the Cuban Crisis, Dominican Republic, NATO, Lebanon, Grenada and the Persian Gulf War. It is now based at Camp Lejeune, North Carolina.

L3: Recon Battalion
Formed in April 1958, it served in the Vietnam War, SEATO, and company elements served in the Per-

In the 1990s some division recon battalions have adopted the LAV25, shown here in Somalia, in a return to the mobility of the 1940s, and others formed into regimental recon companies. (Dawson)

sian Gulf War. It is now based overseas in the Western Pacific.

L4: 4th Recon Battalion
Formed in July 1962 as a reserve unit with companies throughout the United States. A 5th Reconnaissance Battalion was also formed in 1966 and had company elements in the Vietnam War.

Notes sur les planches en couleur

A1 Uniforme 'utility' uni M41 (uniforme de combat et de travail) avec insigne USMC sur la poche de poitrine; casque M1 nouvellement distribué; ceinture M37 pour fusiliers automatiques et Browning Automatic Rifle M1918. **A2** En l'absence d'un uniforme plus pratique il porte l'uniforme khaki avec ceinture à pistolet M36 et gamelle M10; l'arme est le Springfield M1903 avec lunettes téléscopiques. **A3** Dans une mission de reconnaissance sur plage il porte une housse de camouflage de casque comme couvre-chef avec uniforme camouflage M43, ceinture M23, sac premiers secours M42 et tire des fusils Garand M1 de l'écoutille d'un sous-marin.

B1 Unité mixte avec du matériel de l'armée, de la marine, de l'armée de l'air: uniforme M44, bonnet de laine, gants modifiés, corde, gants de travail en cuir, ceinture à cartouches avec couteau en K, boussole, coupe-fils M38, pantalons de toile, fusil M1. **B2** casque M1, pull-over de l'armée, pantalon M41, fusil M1903 avec lunette téléscopique Unertl, couteau M3, grenade Mk.2. **B3** l'uniforme de camouflage M44 était porté presque exclusivement par les unités de reconnaissance en Corée, ici avec le côté marron à l'extérieur bien que la housse de casque soit mise avec le vert à l'extérieur. Remarquez les chevrons de rang à l'encre, le fusil M1, le paquetage M41, l'outil à tranchées M43.

C1 Ce nageur porte une combinaison, un masque et des palmes, une ceinture à pistolet avec un couteau. Des sacs étanches étient utilisés pour porter le reste du

Farbtafeln

A1 Einfache 'Utility'-Uniform M41 (Gefechts- und Arbeitsanzug) mit dem USMC-Abzeichen auf der Brusttasche; neu ausgegebener M1-Helm; M37-Gürtel für Schützen mit Automatikwaffen und M1918 *Browning Automatic Rifle*. **A2** Da es an einer praktischeren Ausrüstung fehlt, trägt er die khakifarbene Dienstuniform mit dem M36-Pistolengürtel und der M10-Feldflasche; bei der Waffe handelt es sich um die M1903 Springfield mit Zielfernrohr. **A3** Bei einer Erkundungsmission am Strand trägt er über dem Helm einen Tarnüberzug, die M43-Tarnuniform, den M23-Gürtel, die M42-Erste-Hilfe-Tasche und hebt M1 Garand-Gewehre aus der Luke eines Unterseeboots.

B1 Die Einheit mit unterschiedlichen Aufgaben macht sich die Ausrüstung der Armee, der Marine und der Luftwaffe zunutze: M44-Uniform, Wollmütze, abgeänderte Handschuhe, Seile, Patronengürtel mit 'K-Bar'-Messer, Kompaß, M38-Drahtschere, Baumwollhosen, M1-Gewehr. **B2** M1-Helm, Armeepullover, M41-Hosen, M1903 Gewehr mit *Unertl-Zielfernrohr*, M3-Messer, Mk.2-Granate. **B3** Die M44-Tarnuniform wurde fast ausschließlich von Spähtrupps in Korea getragen, hier ist sie mit der braunen Seite nach außen abgebildet, obwohl der Helmbezug auf der grünen Seite getragen wird. Man beachte die mit Tusche aufgetragenen Rangwinkel, das M1-Gewehr, den M41-Verpackungssack und das M43-Werkzeug zum Bau von Schützengräben.

matériel. **C2** Les unités de reconnaissance marines adoptèrent du matériel SCUBA pour qu'ils puissent nager depuis le sous-marin pour effectuer la reconnaissance des plages. Le masque était d'origine commerciale. **C3** Pour les missions à l'intérieur des terres les nageurs portaient des sacs étanches et nageaient dans une combinaison. Remarquez la mitraillette M3.

D1 Monteur de parachute faisant la démonstration du parachute T10 modifié pour l'insertion chute libre du personnel de reconnaissance, paquetage sous les cordes de gauche; 'utilities' M58 et bottes Corcoran étient l'uniforme de caserne. Pour le saut, des casques de moto ou de football étaient souvent utilisés. **D2** Uniforme de jungle premier modèle et premières bottes de jungle; fusil M14; mélange de matériel M41; M56 et M61, selon les goûts. Le manque de camouflage et de sacs à dos montre qu'il s'agit d'une répétition et pas d'une mission. **D3** Conseiller avec troupes locles Provisional Reconnaissance Unit portant un uniforme tigré teint en noir, matériel de sanglage M56, carabine CAR-15 alors rare et radio PRC25.

E1 L'uniforme de camouflage et les bottes de jungle ERDL étaient commus dans toute la III Marine Amphibious Force à cette époque. Remarquez le sac à dos ARVN, les deux bidons d'eau d'un litre et le fusil M16 avec sac à munitions 20 balles. **E2** Inspecté avant un saut orienteur en ligne statique, il porte un uniforme en satin M62, un casque de moto, un parachute T10 et un sac de matériel CWIE avec corde. **E3** pour les sauts en forêt et descendre des arbres à la corde, le personnel de reconnaissance portait des combinaisons moletonnées, des casques avec protection du visage des cordes de rappel et les parachutes MC1-1 avec harnais à dégagement rapide.

F1 Les vêtements chauds avaient peu changé depuis la Corée mais étaient maintenant améliorés. Bonnet de laine, parka arctique avec capuche, bottes isolées, les bandes blanches camouflent le fusil M16 et le matériel porte charge ALICE. **F2** Dans les mers chaudes il porte un uniforme de camouflage à la place d'une combinaison, un gilet de sauvetage UDT amélioré, des palmes 'Rocket' et son fusil et attaché à son épaule droite. Les appareils de respiration en circuit ouvert sont encore en opération limitée. **F3** Les shorts khaki 'UDT' étaient une option pour la nage. Les maillots de corps avec insigne d'unité étaient achetés en privé.

G1 Uniforme de camouflage standard pour tout l'USMC à cette date, porté avec matériel de sanglage LC2, chapeau de brousse, gants pour protéger les mains des épines. Remarquez la mitraillette MP5 avec silencieux. **G2** La mission de lutte anti-terroriste et de parachute en chute libre exigent toutes les deux cette tenue: casque de cuir avec bouteille d'oxygène et masque pour les sauts en haute altitude, uniforme de camouflage 'forêt', gants de vol; sanglage '782'; harnais de parachute MT1X; masque à gaz M17 sur la hanche; paquetage entre les jambes; mitraillette MP5. **G3** appareil de respiration LAR-5. Draeger évolué à circuit fermé, porté avec combinaison de plongeur de combat 'Viking'.

H1 Uniforme nommé 'ghillie suit' (nom qui vient des garde-chasse écossais) réalisé par les franc-tireurs à partir de vêtements de camouflage sur lesquels on attachat des bandes de jute et traités anti-détection infrâ-rouge. Fusil M40 avec lunette télescopique Unertl M10. **H2** Pur 'l'Operation Sharp Edge', évacuation des ressortissants américains du Libéria déchiré par la guerre, il porte une 'uniforme ninja' basse visibilité en Goretex avec matériel de sanglage en nylon noir commercial et un pistolet automatique calibre 45. Cet uniforme comportait aussi un sac d'assaut, une capuche et des gants antiflamme, des renforts aux genoux et aux coudes, des lunettes et un casque léger. **H3** Uniforme de camouflage désert standard avec appareil de vision de nuit PVS7, sac ALICE avec radio PR77, matériel de sanglage LC2 et fusil M16A2 avec lunette 'Aimpoint'.

I1 Marine diplômé sortant de l'école de parachutisme grecque, en uniforme de service léger 'toutes saisons'. Badge de parachutiste Navy/Marine sur la poitrine gauche avec rubans amédailles et badge de qualification de tir; badge de parachutiste grec sur la droite. **I2** 'Utilities' et 'cover' (bonnet) de camouflage standard portés avec des bottes et un maillot de corps vert et des insignes de rang et de qualification, même dans les casernes comme tous les jours. **I3** Depuis 1982 on portait des brassards amovibles pour les missions multinationales. Après 1991 l'USMC adopta enfin le port du nom sur la poitrine, dans le même style que les autres services.

J Insignes d'épaule des divisions et autres grandes unités ont été portées durant la guerre mais rarement en dehors des conflits. En 1943–47 les unités de reconnaissance portaient celles du bataillonet de la compagnie de reconnaissance V Amphibious Corps (**J1**) et les six compagnies de reconnaissance (**J2–J7**). Utilisation non officielle des motifs Raider et Parachute de la division se poursuit jusqu'à nos jours par les unités de reconnaissance.

K1 Les Recon Marines n'ont pas d'insignes distinctives mais sont identifiés par leur port des badges de qualification de plongeur SCUBA de la Navy et de parachutiste de l'armée. **K2** Emblèmes non officiels fabriqués sur place des unités reconnaissance Force, comportant souvent des motifs parachutiste et nageur sous-marin.

L Emblèmes non-officiels des unités de reconnaissance Division, comportant souvent les anciens motifs divisionnels de la seconde guerre mondiale, le motif 'Billy Bones' des anciens Raider Battalions et autres variations.

C1 Dieser Schwimmer trägt einen Schwimmanzug, eine Taucherbrille und Schwimmflossen, einen Pistolengürtel mit Messer; die andere Ausrüstung wurde in wasserfesten Taschen mitgeführt. **C2** Spaheinheiten der Marineinfanterie machten sich die SCUBA-Ausrüstung zunutze, so daß sie vom U-Boot aus unter Wasser an den Strand schwimmen konnten; das Atemgerät war kommerzieller Herkunft. **C3** Für Einsätze, die vom Strand wasserfeste Taschen mit sich und schwammen im Tauchanzug. Man benutzte die M3-Maschinenpistole.

D1 Der Fallschirm-Rüstmechaniker demonstriert den 10-Fallschirm, der für den Freifall-Ausstieg von Spähern umgebaut worden war. Der Tornister befindet sich unter den Gurten auf der linken Seite; M58 'Utilities' und Corcoran-Springerstiefel gehörten zur Kasernenkleidung. Beim Absprung trug man oft Motorrad- oder Football-Helme. **D2** Erstes Muster der Dschungeluniform und frühe Dschungelstiefel; M14-Gewehr; Kombination der individuellen Ausrüstung der Stile M41, M56 und M61 je nach Geschmack. Das Fehlen der Tarnung und des Rucksacks macht deutlich, daß es sich hier um eine Probeübung handelt, und nicht um einen Einsatz. **D3** Berater mit örtlichen Provisional Reconnaissance Unit portant un uniforme in schwarz gefärbter Tigerstreifen-Uniform, M56-Gurtausrüstung, dem damals seltenen CAR-15-Karabiner und dem PRC25-Funkgerät.

E1 Die ERDL-Tarnuniform und die Dschungelstiefel gehörten zu dieser Zeit bei der gesamten III Marine Amphibious Force zur Standardausrüstung; man beachte den ARVN-Rucksack, die 2-Liter-Wasserfeldflaschen und das M16-Gewehr mit einem 20-Runden-Magazin. **E2** Bei der Inspektion vor einem Pfadfinderabsprung in Reihe trägt er die M62-'Utility'-Uniform aus Baumwollsatin, einen Motorradhelm, den T10-Fallschirm und die CWIE-Ausrüstungstasche mit Ablaßseil. **E3** Für den Absprung in Waldgebieten und das Abseilen aus den Baumkronen hatten die Spähtrupps wattierte Overalls, Helme mit Gesichtsschutz und Seile; MC1-1-Fallschirm mit Schnellauslöser-Gurtzeug.

F1 Die Kleidung für kaltes Wetter hatte sich seit Korea kaum geändert, wurde jedoch nun verbessert. Wollmütze, warmer Anorak mit Kapuze, Gerätezugzeug **F2** In warmen Gewässern trägt er eine Tarnuniform anstatt des Tauchanzugs, die verbesserte UDT-Schwimmweste, 'Rocket'-Schwimmflossen, und sein Gewehr ist an der rechten Schulter befestigt. Das Atemgerät mit offenem Sauerstoffkreislauf behinderte die Einsätz noch. **F3** Khakifarbene 'UDT'-Shorts wurden wahlweise zum Schwimmen getragen; Unterhemden mit dem Abzeichen der Einheit wurden privat gekauft.

G1 Die Tarnuniform gehörte zu dieser Zeit bei der USMC zur Standardausgabe und wurde mit LC2-Gurtausrüstung, Dschungelhut und Handschuhen zum Schutz vor Dornen getragen; man beachte die MP5-Maschinenpistole mit Schalldämpfer. **G2** Der Terrorabwehreinsatz und das Abspringen im freien Fall machen diese Aufmachung nötig: Lederhelm mit Sauerstofflasche und Maske für Sprünge aus großer Höhe; 'Wald'-Tarnuniform; Fliegerhandschuhe; '782'-Gurtzeug, MT1X-Fallschirmgurtzeug, M17-Gasmaske an der Hüfte, Verpackungssack zwischen den Beinen; MP5-Maschinenpistole. **G3** Technisch fortgeschrittenes LAR-5 Draeger-Atemgerät mit geschlossenem Sauerstoffkreislauf, das mit 'Viking'-Kampftauchanzug getragen wird.

H1 Der sogenannte 'Ghillie Suit' (nach schottischen Wildhütern benannt) wurde von Heckenschützen aus Tarnkleidung gemacht, an die Sackleinenstücke angebracht wurden, und wurde auf Anti-Infrarotentdeckung behandelt. M40-Gewehr mit M10 Unertl-Zielfernrohr. **H2** Bei der 'Operation Sharp Edge', d.h. der Evakuierung amerikanischer Bürger aus dem kriegszerrütteten Liberia, trägt er einen Goretex-'Ninja-Anzug', der schwer zu entdecken ist, sowie schwarzes Nylon-Gurtzeug kommerzieller Herkunft und eine 45er Automatikpistole. Zu dieser Aufmachung gehörte außerdem ein Sturmangriffsack, eine feuerfeste Kapuze und Handschuhe, Polster an den Ellbogen und den Knien, eine Schutzbrille und leichter Helm. **H3** PRC77-Funkgerät, LC2-Gurtzeug und das M16A2-Gewehr mit 'Aimpoint' Zielfernrohr.

I1 Marineinfanterist nach Absolvierung der griechischen Fallschirmspringerschule in leichtem 'Allwetter'-Dienstanzug. Fallschirmspringerabzeichen der Marine-Marineinfanterie auf der linken Brustseite mit Medaillenbändern und dem Schützenabzeichen; das griechische Fallschirmspringerabzeichen auf der rechten Seite. **I2** Standardmäßige Tarn-'Utilities' und 'Cover' (Mütze), die mit Stiefeln und grünem Unterhemd getragen wurden, sowie Rang- und Qualifizierungsabzeichen waren selbst in der Kaserne die Alltagskleidung. **I3** Seit 1982 werden bei multinationalen Einsätzen die abnehmbaren Armelfähnchen getragen; ab 1991 ging auch die USMC zu den Namensbändern auf der Brust über, die in der Machart denen der anderen Einheiten glichen.

J Schulterabzeichen der Divisionen und anderen großen Einheiten wurden zu Kriegszeiten aber ansonsten selten getragen. 1943–46 trugen die Spähtrupps das Abzeichen des Erkundungsbataillons und -kompanie des V Amphibious Corps (**J1**) und der sechs Divisionsspähtrupps (**J2–J7**). Bis heute tragen Spähtrupps inoffiziell die Motive der Divisionen Raider und Parachute.

K1 Recon Marines haben kein charakteristisches Abzeichen, sondern sind durch die Qualifikationsabzeichen des Marine-SCUBA-Tauchers und des Armee Fallschirmspringers erkenntlich. **K2** Auf den inoffiziellen, örtlich hergestellten Abzeichen der Force-Spähtrupps sieht man oft Fallschirm- und Unterwasserschwimmer-Motive.

L Auf den inoffiziellen Abzeichen der Spähtrupps der Division sieht man häufig alten Divisionsmotive aus dem zweiten Weltkrieg, das 'Billy Bones'-Motiv der alten Raider Battalions sowie unterschiedliche variationen.